British and Irish FOLK TALES

Folktales, Myths and Legends by the same author

Axe-Age, Wolf-Age: A selection from the Norse Myths
Beowulf
British Folk Tales
The Dead Moon: Tales from East Anglia and the Fen Country
The Faber Book of Northern Folk Tales (Editor)
The Faber Book of Northern Legends (Editor)
Northern Lights: Legends, Sagas and Folktales (Editor)
The Mabinogion (with Gwyn Thomas)
The Quest for Olwen (with Gwyn Thomas)

British and Irish FOLK TALES

A Selection of Stories from British Folk Tales

Kevin Crossley-Holland

Chapter Headings by Peter Melnyczuk

ORCHARD BOOKS

"The Green Children" and "The Dauntless Girl" and "The Pedlar of Swaffham" are reprinted from *The Dead Moon* (André Deutsch 1982). *The Wildman* was first published by André Deutsch in 1976.

This selection first published in Great Britain in 1990

ORCHARD BOOKS
96 Leonard Street, London EC2A 4RH

Orchard Books Australia
14 Mars Road, Lane Cove, NSW 2066

1 85213 265 5

Made and printed in Great Britain by
The Guernsey Press Co. Ltd., Guernsey, Channel Islands.

CONTENTS

THE LAMBTON WORM

Childe Lambton never went to Mass on Sunday mornings.

"Think of your position," said his father.

"You go your way," said the Childe, "and I'll go mine."

"Think of your soul," said Lord Lambton.

But next Sunday was no different. While Lord Lambton and all the servants at the Hall and the workers on the estate crossed the bridge over the Wear, and made their way into the Lambton chapel, the Childe went fishing.

The young man whistled and pulled on his waders. He sidestepped down the steep river bank. He stood in a pool of golden light and cast his line into the laughing water.

"Hell!" swore the Childe when his hook snagged a lump of sodden weed, and "Hell!" when an hour had passed, dark and swift, and he had still caught nothing, not even a tiddler.

The water glittered. The young man screwed up his eyes and cast his line once more, and then at once he saw the float disappear and felt a great tug at his line. He played his catch and began to haul it in.

The Childe was astonished at the sight of his catch. The creature on the hook looked more like a lizard or a small snake than a fish. It was at least one foot long, with nine holes on either side of its mouth, and dry-skinned and scaly.

"Hell!" shouted the Childe. "Hell and damnation! What in God's name is this?"

"What's wrong?" said a voice.

The Childe spun round and up above him was an old man, his face acorn-brown and his clothes in tatters.

"What have you caught?" the old man called. "Swearing like that! And on a Sunday!"

"Look!" said the Childe. "I think I've caught the devil himself."

The old man levered himself down the bank and stared at the creature. "You have and all," he said.

"Do you recognise him then?" said the Childe, grinning.

"It's wicked," said the old man, "whatever it is. And it won't do you no good, that's for sure."

"Finished?" said the Childe, and he looked at the creature that was lashing its tail and trying to get off the hook.

"Don't you throw him back," said the old man. "You caught him and you keep him." And with that, he turned his back on the Childe, hauled himself up the bank, and went on his way.

Childe Lambton stared at the wriggling creature and with its cold, glassy eyes the creature stared at him.

"Gruesome," said the Childe. "That's what you are. And I know what I can do with you."

Still holding his rod, and the creature attached to it, the Childe climbed up the river bank and strode to the nearby well.

"Gruesome!" said the Childe. "And I never want to see you again." Then he grasped the creature's dry skin, and unhooked it, and tossed it into the well.

Time passed and the creature grew too large to live in the well. One spring morning it stuck out its head and blinked its lidless eyes; it opened its mouth and roared!

A half-grown worm, it thrust up and out, and shrithed down to the river. It coiled itself around a rock out in the quick water.

But that night the worm left the river and went visiting. It wrapped itself around a cow and sucked her dry. It chased five skipping lambs and ate them. It snarled and hissed in the darkness and terrified the workers on the estate and the servants in the Hall.

In the early hours, the worm sidled and slid to a nearby hill and wound itself three times round it. There it rested until daybreak. But then it made its way back to the river and the whole dreadful cycle began again.

Childe Lambton went to Mass; every day he went and on his knees prayed that they should all be delivered from the worm. The young man did penance. But now the worm attacked calves and sheep, and lashed its tail, and every night the darkness was filled with terrible noises.

"If I leave this district," said the Childe, "will the worm leave it too? I'll go on a pilgrimage to the Holy Land; then God may forgive me and spare us all this terrible scourge."

The Childe was as good as his word. Only a few days

later, he said a sad farewell to his father and set off from the Hall. Then at once the worm's behaviour changed; but far from leaving old Lord Lambton in peace, it grew even more dangerous and daring. In the evening it crossed the fields between the River Wear and Lambton Hall, and slowly shrithed up towards the Hall itself. Inside the Hall, the servants were terrified. The men picked up kitchen knives and cudgels, the dogs barked and barked, and in the stables the horses neighed and whinnied in terror.

One old steward kept his head. "Milk!" he said. "I've heard that worms drink milk." He hurried across to the dairy and found the two dairymaids there. "Bring out the milk!" he ordered. "Every pail! As quick as you can!"

Lifting two pails himself, the steward led the way to the stone trough in front of the Hall. He poured the frothing milk straight into it, and the dairymaids followed him. In all, they poured the milk from nine cattle into the trough.

The worm crossed the physick garden and the rose garden, and nosed its way up to the trough. It sniffed at the milk and at once began to lap it up. Splashing and slurping, it drank until it had drained the trough dry, and then it shot out its forked tongue and licked the stone. After this, the worm turned away from the Hall; it lumbered away to the hill, and wrapped itself around it, and settled down for the night.

From that day on, the steward made sure that the trough was filled each evening with the milk of nine cattle. When once several of the cattle fell sick, and did not produce much milk, the worm hissed and snarled. It shrithed round the park, lashing its tail in fury, and uprooted two huge oaks and a fir tree.

The seasons turned and the years passed, and one knight and then another and then a third came to the help of Lord

Lambton. Each was sure he could kill the worm, and win fame and a name for ever. But all three knights came to the same end. The worm coiled itself around them, one by one, and squeezed them to death.

For seven years Childe Lambton did penance in the Holy Land and at the end of the seventh year he came home.

The young man saw that the fields around the Hall had not been ploughed and in the corner of one field stood a ploughshare, rusty. The paddocks once full of bullocks and lambs were deserted. No brazen pheasants were lording it on the lawns. Many of the park trees had been uprooted. The Childe looked about him in utter dismay.

Inside the Hall, the Childe found his old father, grown white with time and frail with worry. The Hall itself was webbed and dusty. For fear of the worm, every single servant except the faithful steward had fled from the place.

The Childe took his father into his arms.

"I forgive you," said the old man, trembling.

"Oh! Father!" said the Childe.

"Will you go and see the wise woman at Brugeford?" said the old man. "Will you ask her if there is anything at all you can do to save us from this worm?"

When Childe Lambton had found the wise woman, she told him at once: "You brought this on our heads, and only you can release us."

"I'd lay down my life to spare my father more suffering," the young man said.

"Maybe you will," said the wise woman. "But you, and only you, can kill this worm."

"How?" asked the Childe.

"Take your suit of armour to the blacksmith. Have him

spike it. Ask him to inlay it with sharp spear-points. Then, before dawn, go down to the river. Wait for the worm there."

"I will," said the Childe.

"There's one thing more," added the wise woman. "You must swear an oath that, if you kill the worm, you'll put to death the first living thing you meet on your way back to the Hall. Do this, and all will be well. Fail, and the Lambtons will be cursed. No Lambton will die in peace, in his own bed, for nine generations."

"I swear," said the Childe.

Childe Lambton went straight back to the Hall to report what the wise woman had said.

"If I kill this worm," the Childe said, "I'll blow my bugle three times. If you hear three blasts, open the doors and let Tempest run out to me."

Tempest wagged his tail at the sound of his name.

"Whatever you do," said the Childe, "be sure not to come out before the dog does. There's no other way to do it," he muttered.

Then Childe Lambton went to the forge and, when the smith had inlaid his armour with vicious spikes, he withdrew to the chapel at Brugeford. He prayed and renewed his vow, and before dawn he donned his armour and went down to the river.

As soon as darkness paled, the worm shrithed from the hill towards the water, and swam up the river towards the weeping rock. At once it saw the Childe. It rapped the water with its tail and raised a sheet of flying spray. Then the worm snarled and surged forward; it seized the young man and wound its coils around him and tried to crush him to death.

But the tighter the worm squeezed, the more fiercely the

spear-points dug into its flesh. The worm hissed; the river darkened.

Then the worm eased its grip; it unwound its coils. As soon as his right arm was free, the Childe raised his sword. He crashed it down: with one savage blow he cut the creature in half.

The tail end of the worm was at once swept away in the dark waters. But its head and body renewed the attack, and again coiled round the Childe in his armour. Once more the spear-points did their worst. Poisonous blood spurted into the river and, when it unwound itself for a second time, the worm was too weak to fight any longer. Its eyes were bleary. It slumped into the water, coughing foam and blood; and as the hurrying current took it, it rolled over on to its back and died.

The Childe raised his visor and staggered up the river bank. In his armour he walked across the wrecked park and into the rose garden. There he raised his bugle to his lips and blew three resounding blasts.

The old lord and the steward stared at each other. They grasped each other's arms. In their excitement they forgot what they were meant to do and swung open the Hall doors and hurried out first themselves.

Childe Lambton grasped his sword, still dripping with the worm's blood. He stared at his father, horrified. "The oath! The oath!" he shouted. And he raised his bugle and blew another blast.

The old lord and his steward stopped in their tracks. For a moment they stood there and then they turned away. They stumbled back through the doors and untied Tempest.

The young man's loyal hound came bounding out to meet him. Then the Childe pursed his lips; he swung his sword and lopped off Tempest's head.

Childe Lambton had killed the worm, and seven years of terror were at an end; but he had broken his vow, and one curse was replaced by another. No Lambton died in peace, in his own bed, for nine generations.

TOM TIT TOT

There was once a little old village where a woman lived with her giddy daughter. The daughter was just sixteen, and sweet as honey-suckle.

One fine morning, the woman made five meat pies and put them in the oven. But then a neighbour called round and they were soon so busy with snippets of gossip that the woman completely forgot about the pies. By the time she took them out of the oven, their crusts were almost as hard as the bark of her old oak tree.

"Daughter," she said, "you put them there pies in the larder."

"My! I'm that hungry," said the girl.

"Leave them there and they'll come again."

"Come again?"

"You know," said the woman. And she hurried out into the warm wind and her waiting neighbour.

"Well!" said the girl. "If they'll come again, I'll eat these now." And so she went back to the larder and picked up the pies and ate them all, first and last.

When it was supper time, the woman felt very hungry. "I could just do with one of them there pies," she said. "Go and get one off the shelf. They'll have come again now."

The girl went and looked in the larder, and there was nothing on the shelf but an empty dish. "No!" she called. "They haven't."

"Not none of them?" said the woman.

"No!" the girl called. "No! Not none."

"Well!" said the woman. "Come again or not, I'll have one for my supper."

"You can't if they haven't come," said the girl, walking out of the larder.

"I can though," said the woman. "Go and get the best one."

"Best or worst," said the girl, "I've eaten the lot, so you can't have one till that's come again."

The woman was furious. "Eaten the lot!" she cried. "You dardledumdue!"

The woman carried her spinning wheel over to the door and, to calm herself, she began to spin. As she spun she sang:

"My daughter's ate five; five pies today.
My daughter's ate five; five pies today."

The king came walking down the street and heard the woman. "What were those words, woman?" he asked. "What were you singing?"

The woman felt ashamed of her daughter's greed. "Well!" she said, beginning to spin again:

"My daughter's spun five; five skeins today.
My daughter's spun five; five skeins today."

"Stars of mine!" exclaimed the king. "I've never heard of anyone who could do that." The king raised his eyebrows and looked at the girl, so sweet and giddy and sixteen; he stared at a flowerbed and rubbed his nose.

"Five today," said the woman.

"Look here!" said the king. "I want a wife and I'll marry your daughter. For eleven months of the year," he said, "she can eat as much food as she likes, and buy all the dresses she wants; she can keep whatever company she wishes. But during the last month of the year, she'll have to spin five skeins every day; and if she doesn't, I'll cut off her head."

"All right!" said the woman. "That's all right, isn't it, daughter?"

The woman was delighted at the thought that her daughter was going to marry the king himself. She wasn't worried about the five skeins. "When that comes to it," she told her daughter later, "we'll find a way out of it. More likely, though, he'll have clean forgot about it."

So the king and the girl were married. And for eleven months the girl ate as much food as she liked and bought all the dresses she wanted and kept whatever company she wished.

As the days of the eleventh month passed, the girl began to think about those skeins and wondered whether the king was thinking about them too. But the king said not a word, and the girl almost sure he had completely forgotten them.

On the very last day of the month, though, the king led

her up to a room in the palace she had never set eyes on before. There was nothing in it but a spinning wheel and a stool.

"Now, my dear," said the king, "you'll be shut in here tomorrow with some food and flax. And if you haven't spun five skeins before dark, your head will be cut off."

Then away went the king to do everything a king has to do.

Well, the girl was that frightened. She had always been such a giddy girl, and she didn't know how to spin. She didn't know what to do next morning, with no one beside her and no one to help her. She sat down on a stool in the palace kitchen and heavens! how she did cry.

All of a sudden, however, she heard a sort of knocking low down on the door. So she stood up and opened the door, and what did she see but a small little black thing with a long tail. It looked up at her, all curious, and it said, "Well! What are you crying for?"

"What's that to you?" sobbed the girl.

"Never you mind," it said. "You tell me what you're crying for."

"That won't do me no good if I do," the girl replied.

"You don't know that," it said, and twirled its tail round.

"Well!" she said. "That won't do me no harm if that don't do me no good." So she told him about the pies and the skeins and everything.

"This is what I'll do," said the little black thing. "I'll come to your window every morning and take the flax; and I'll bring it back all spun before dark."

"What will that cost me?" she asked.

The thing looked out of the corners of its eyes and it

said, "Every night I'll give you three guesses at my name. And if you haven't guessed it before the month's up, you shall be mine."

Well, she thought she was bound to guess its name before the month was out. "All right," she said. "I agree to that."

"All right!" it said, and lork! how it twirled its tail.

Well, next morning, the king led the girl up to the room, and the flax and the day's food were all ready for her.

"There's the flax," said her husband, "and if it isn't spun before dark, off goes your head!" Then he went out and locked the door.

The king had scarcely gone out when there was a knocking at the window.

The girl stood up and opened it and, sure enough, there was the little old thing sitting on the window ledge.

"Where's the flax?" it said.

"Here it is!" she said.

Well, when it was early evening, there was a knocking again at the window. The girl stood up and opened it, and there was the little old thing, with five skeins of flax over his arm.

"Here it is!" it said, and it gave the flax to her. "And now," it said, "what's my name?"

"What, is that Bill?" she said.

"No!" it said, "that ain't." And it twirled its tail.

"Is that Ned?" she said.

"No!" it said, "that ain't." And it twirled its tail.

"Well, is that Mark?" said she.

"No!" it said, "that ain't." And it twirled its tail faster, and away it flew.

Well, when the girl's husband came in, the five skeins

were ready for him. "I see I shan't have to kill you tonight, my dear," he said. "You'll have your food and your flax in the morning," he said, and away he went to do everything a king has to do.

Well, the flax and the food were made ready for the girl each day, and each day the little black impet used to come in the morning and return in the early evening. And each day and all day the girl sat thinking of names to try out on the impet when he came back in the evening. But she never hit on the right one! As time went on towards the end of the month, the impet looked wickeder and wickeder, and it twirled its tail faster and faster each time she made a guess.

So they came to the last day of the month but one. The impet returned in the early evening with the five skeins, and it said, "What, hain't you guessed my name yet?"

"Is that Nicodemus?" she said.

"No! 't'ain't," it said.

"Is that Samuel?" she said.

"No! 't'ain't," it said.

"Ah! well. Is that Methusalem?" said she.

"No! 't'ain't that either," it said. And then it looked at the girl with eyes like burning coals.

"Woman," it said, "there's only tomorrow evening, and then you'll be mine!" And away it flew!

Well, the girl felt terrible. Soon, though, she heard the king coming along the passage; and when he had walked into the room and seen the five skeins, he said, "Well, my dear! So far as I can see, you'll have your skeins ready tomorrow evening too. I reckon I won't have to kill you, so I'll have my supper in here tonight." So the king's servants brought up his supper, and another stool for him, and the two of them sat down together.

Well, the king had scarcely eaten a mouthful before he pushed back his stool, and waved his knife and fork, and began to laugh.

"What is it?" asked the girl.

"I'll tell you," said the king. "I was out hunting today, and I got lost and came to a clearing in the forest I'd never seen before. There was an old chalkpit there. And I heard a kind of sort of humming. So I got off my horse and crept up to the edge of the pit and looked down into it. And do you know what I saw? The funniest little black thing you ever set eyes on! And what did it have but a little spinning wheel! It was spinning and spinning, wonderfully fast, spinning and twirling its tail. And as it spun, it sang,

"Nimmy nimmy not,
My name's Tom Tit Tot."

Well, when the girl heard this, she could have jumped out of her skin for joy; but she didn't say a word.

Next morning, the small little black thing looked wicked as wicked when it came for the flax. And just before it grew dark, she heard it knocking again at the window pane. She opened the window and it came right in on to the sill. It was grinning from ear to ear, and ooh! its tail was twirling round so fast.

"What's my name?" it said, as it gave her the skeins.

"Is that Solomon?" she said, pretending to be afraid.

"No! 't'ain't," it said, and it came further into the room.

"Well, is that Zebedee?" she said again.

"No! 't'ain't," said the impet. And then it laughed and twirled its tail until you could scarcely see it.

"Take time, woman," it said. "Next guess, and you're mine." And it stretched out its black hands towards her.

Well, the girl backed away a step or two. She looked at it, and then she laughed and pointed a finger at it and sang out:

"Nimmy nimmy not,
Your name's Tom Tit Tot."

Well, when the impet heard her, it gave an awful shriek and away it flew into the dark. She never saw it again.

MONDAY, TUESDAY

Poor Lusmore! He was all misshapen. His legs were bowed, and the hump on his back was as big as a football. When he stood up, he seemed almost to be squatting; and when he sat down, he rested his chin on his knees for support.

Lusmore's arms, though, were strong and tanned, and his fingers were nimble. Almost every day he sat on his low stool outside the cottage where he lived with his old parents — he was almost thirty himself — and plaited rushes and straw into baskets and hats. And he always got a good price for his work because everyone felt so sorry for him.

Everyone talked about him too, of course! Out of his hearing, people said all kinds of things about Lusmore. They said no human being could be as deformed as he was, and that he must be a changeling. They said he warbled strange words to himself. They said he was a master of magic and medicine.

Lusmore seemed unaware of all this. His daily suffering had made him gentle and sweet. He was glad he was alive. He loved birds and butterflies. Every morning in summer, he tucked a foxglove through the band of his straw hat, and sang as he worked, and eagerly greeted each and every passer-by.

One day, Lusmore rode on the back of a cart into the town of Caher, and sold his baskets and hats in the market there. He did a brisk trade, and went off to drink a few beers afterwards. But when he returned to the deserted market-place, it was late, the light was failing, and the cart and its driver were nowhere to be seen. Poor Lusmore! He had no choice but to walk home.

The little hunchback trudged out of Caher down the road towards Cappagh, and by the time he reached the old moat at Knockgrafton it was already quite dark. Lusmore hauled his sad shape of a body off the road and over the molehills and tussocks and sat down on the edge of the old grassy ditch.

"And I'm not halfway home," said Lusmore, and he gave a great sigh—the kind he only permitted himself when no one else was nearby.

The hunchback sat cross-legged, his chin resting on one knee, and looked at the gibbous moon. Lumpen clouds were swarming over it, and it seemed as if the moon were running, or rolling as fast as she could without getting anywhere.

"Like me!" said Lusmore, and he smiled ruefully. "Just like me! I'm a poor moon-calf."

Lusmore pressed his chin against his knee and closed his eyes. He listened to the shushing of the light wind in the old lime trees down the road; and then he heard rising above the wind and out of the grassy moat a different sound, clearer and higher in pitch — a song without words. It was the sound of many voices, sweet voices, so mingling and blending that they sounded like one voice. Then the voices began to sing words: "Monday, Tuesday, Monday, Tuesday, Monday, Tuesday . . ." At this, they paused for a moment, and then they began the melody again.

Lusmore was spellbound by the singing. *Though to be sure*, he thought to himself, *there's not much variety to it.* After a while, the hunchback began to hum the melody in tune with the voices; and then, when they paused, he sang out "Wednesday".

"Monday, Tuesday . . ." sang the voices and Lusmore sang with them, "Monday, Tuesday, Monday, Tuesday . . ." And then, for a second time, "Wednesday".

When the little people heard Lusmore, they were delighted. They skipped and eddied up the bank, and swirled him down to the bottom of the moat in a whirlwind of cries and laughter. The hunchback was twirled round and round, light as a piece of straw, and the fairy fiddlers played faster and faster.

When the world stopped spinning, Lusmore saw he had been swept into a fine fairy pavilion. True, it was rather low ceilinged, but that didn't bother him! The whole place was lit with candles and packed out with little people — little people chattering, eating, playing fiddles and pipes and harps, dancing . . .

Lusmore was made most welcome: he was given a low stool, and provided with food and drink.

"Grand! I feel grand!" he said as one fairy after another enquired whether he had all he needed, and praised his skill as a singer. "Just grand!" said Lusmore. "I might as well be the king of the whole land!"

Then the music faltered and stopped; the dancers stood still; the feasters put down their knives and forks. Lusmore watched as the little people crowded together in the middle of the pavilion, and began to whisper. Now the hunchback began to feel nervous: "For all your kindness and courtesy," he muttered, "you fairy folk, you're fickle and chancy."

As Lusmore watched, one little man left the huddle and walked up to him. He smiled at Lusmore and solemnly he said:

"Lusmore! Lusmore!
That hump you wore,
That hump you bore
On your back is no more;
Look down on the floor!
There's your hump, Lusmore!"

As the hunchback looked down, his ugly hump fell from his shoulders and dropped to the ground. Little Lusmore felt so light; he felt so happy; like the cow in the story of the cat and the fiddle, he could have jumped over the moon.

But seeing the hump was scarcely enough! Lusmore raised his arms and clasped the back of his neck. Then very slowly, for fear of bumping his head against the ceiling, Lusmore lifted his head. For the first time in his life, he stood upright.

Lusmore laughed and then he cried. The fair pavilion, the little people crowding around him, they were all so beautiful. Lusmore began to feel dizzy; his eyesight became dim; he slipped gently to the ground, and fell fast asleep.

When Lusmore woke, the sun was already well up. The dewy grass . . . cows chewing the cud . . . the moat at Knockgrafton . . . Then he remembered! He crossed himself. And still lying on the grass, he reached out with one hand and felt behind his back.

When Lusmore was sure that the hump was not there, he leaped up. He got down on his knees and said his prayers. Then he saw he was wearing a new suit of clothes, and shook his head, grinning.

So Lusmore stepped out for Cappagh, feeling as light as a piece of thistledown. He had such a spring in his step that you might have thought he had been a dancing-master all his life. His mother and father and all the people living in the village were astonished at the sight of him — indeed at first glance many of them did not even recognise him. And it wasn't long before the story of how Lusmore had lost his hump was taken to Caher, and then spread for miles and miles around; it was soon the talk of everyone in the midlands of Ireland.

Lusmore had learned to live with his misfortune and now he took his good fortune with a shrug and a smile. Free of his ugly load, he delighted in his dapper appearance, but he had no wish to harum-scarum off to Dublin or climb Croagh Patrick or drink himself into an early grave. He was already in the place he loved, and he was among the friends and neighbours he had known since the day of his birth. He went on with his old job of plaiting rushes and straw.

One morning, Lusmore was sitting in the sunlight outside his cottage door when a woman walked up to him.

"This is the road to Cappagh?" she asked.

"This is Cappagh," Lusmore replied. "Who are you looking for?"

"I've come from County Waterford," said the woman. "Over thirty miles. I'm looking for one Lusmore."

"I know him," said Lusmore.

"He had the hump taken off him by the fairies," said the woman. "Is that right?"

"It is," said Lusmore, smiling.

"Well, the son of a neighbour of mine—Jack—Jack Madden the cobbler—he's got a devil of a hump on him. That'll soon be the death of him . . ."

"I am Lusmore," said the little man.

"You!" exclaimed the woman. "Well! There's an omen!"

Lusmore was quite happy to tell the woman what had happened at the old moat at Knockgrafton. He explained about the tune the fairies had sung, and how he had joined in and added to it, and about the fair pavilion, the whispering fairies . . .

The woman thanked Lusmore. She hurried back down the long lanes to her own county. She went straight to her neighbour and it wasn't more than a couple of days before the two of them arranged for a horse and cart to take them and Jack Madden all the way back to Knockgrafton.

On the way there, Jack's mouth was full of complaints. "This jolting," he said. "That'll be the death of me! It's all right for you!" He complained his mother would make him work twice as hard to pay for the cost of the cart. He complained at the taste of the ale they had brought with them. What with his peevishness and the noise of the cart, Jack's mother and her neighbour were worn out by the time they reached the moat at Knockgrafton.

"Don't forget what we've told you," they said. "We'll

be back at sunrise." Then the cart rolled away down the road to Caher and Jack Madden was left on his own in the darkness under the rising moon.

Jack hauled his sad shape of a body off the road and over the molehills and tussocks and sat down on the edge of the old grassy ditch. The stillness of the place wrapped itself round him: the clucking of a bird, settling down for the night; a far barking; acres of silence.

And then, out of this silence, from somewhere down in the moat, rose sweet singing, high-pitched clear singing that made Jack Madden catch his breath and listen intently. The fairies were singing their song just as Lusmore had shaped it for them.

"Monday, Tuesday," they sang, "Monday, Tuesday, Monday, Tuesday, Wednesday." There was no pause in their singing now; the melody and words were continuous.

Jack Madden's spirit was as shapeless as his body. He had no grace about him, and little sense of the fitting. He listened to the little people sing their song seven times and then, without regard for timing and without thought for pitch, he stood up and bawled out, "WEDNESDAY, THURSDAY".

If one day is good, thought Jack, *two days are better. I should get two suits of clothing*!

The fairies whirled up the grassy bank. They lifted Jack off his feet and swept him down to the bottom of the moat and into their pavilion. There they jostled around him, picking at his clothing and banging him with their tiny fists, screeching and screaming "Who spoiled our tune? Who spoiled our tune?"

Then one little man raised his hand and the crowd of angry fairies fell back. The little man narrowed his eyes at Jack and said:

"Jack Madden! Jack Madden!
Your words were all wrong
For our sweet lovely song.
You're caught in our throng
And your life we will sadden:
Here's two lumps for Jack Madden."

At this, a troop of twenty of the strongest fairies staggered into the pavilion, carrying Lusmore's hump. They walked over to poor Jack and at once slammed it down on his back, right over his own hump. And as soon as they had done so, it became firmly fixed there, as if it had been nailed down with six-inch nails by the best of carpenters. Then the little people screeched and screamed again, and kicked Jack out of their pavilion into the dark night.

In the morning, Jack Madden's mother and her neighbour came back from Caher. They found Jack lying just outside the moat, with a double hump on his back; he was half-dead.

The two women looked at him; they looked at each other; but for fear of the fairies, they said nothing. They lifted poor Jack and laid him moaning in the bottom of the cart, and rode straight home to Waterford.

What with the terrible weight of his second hump, and the strain of the long jolting journey, Jack Madden didn't live long. "My curse," he muttered just before he died, "my curse on any fool who listens to a fairy tune!"

THE SLUMBER KING

"Owen," said a voice.

Owen spun round and looked into the bright eyes of a small, boyish-faced, middle-aged man. "Who are you?" he demanded.

"Don't you worry about me," said the man pleasantly. "Loomis. Loomis is the name."

"I mean, how did you know my name?"

"I've been watching you," said the man. "You can tell most things by watching. You've been standing here on London Bridge and your mind has been on a long journey back to your parents, back home to Wales."

"How do you know that?" said Owen, startled.

"And I can tell you this," said the man. "You should value that stick of yours."

Owen looked at his hazel walking-stick; he had cut it from a bush under the Rock of the Fortress and seldom went anywhere without it.

"Under the place where that stick grew," said Loomis, "there's gold in the earth."

"There's gold all over the mountains," said Owen. "Red gold."

"No," said the man. "Right under the place where that stick grew. Do you remember it?"

Owen nodded.

"Take me to it and the gold is yours."

Owen took Loomis with him back to Wales. He led him to his own valley, in the mountains north of Swansea, and they walked past the pool where the rivers Mellte and Sychryd meet, through a rising wood of oak and ash and up to an old hazel bush.

Immediately above it reared the mighty Rock of the Fortress.

"You're sure?" said Loomis.

"This is it," said Owen.

The little man sat down on the carpet of twigs and puzzled with the straps of his canvas bag, and at length he pulled out two spades.

Owen laughed. "You're full of surprises," he said.

"Now," said Loomis. "We've got to dig up this bush."

Under the roots, under all the dark webbing, lay a large flat stone, a little bigger than the cover of a manhole. Owen had to dig wide and deep before he was able to prise it out of the ground. And as it came up, he saw it hid the entrance to a rock passageway.

"Ah!" said Loomis, raising his eyebrows and smiling at Owen agreeably. "Well, shall I lead the way?"

Owen nodded and stepped back.

"Don't you worry!" said Loomis. "I'll tell you what to do, and what not to do." He groped in one pocket, then another, then a third, and fished out two boxes of matches. "You'll need these," he said, handing one box to Owen, "unless you're able to see in the dark."

"Can you?" Owen asked.

"Of course not," said Loomis.

Feet first, Loomis and Owen lowered themselves through the entrance. Then each lit a match and Owen saw rough dank walls and a narrow passageway. Starting forward in Loomis' footsteps, he felt the ground gently falling away under his feet. They were going in under the mountain.

"Watch out for the bell," said Loomis, and now his voice sounded eerie and hollow. "Don't touch it whatever you do."

Owen saw a large bell standing in the middle of the passageway and ducked low under it. Now the passage began to widen and lighten, and suddenly it opened on to a vast cavern. Owen realised that he was standing at the top of a flight of roughly hewn steps, halfway between the cavern roof and floor, and he gazed breathless at the wonders below him.

Thousands of warriors lay there, sleeping. They lay in a huge circle, their feet pointing inwards and their heads outwards. Each warrior was clad in bright armour and by the side of each lay his sword, his lance and his shield.

The whole cavern was brightly lit, as if ten thousand candles were burning in it, and all this light came from the warriors' weapons and war-gear. Chainmail and plated helmets, the blades of battle-axes, spear tips, shield bosses, they all shone with a steady bright light.

Owen stared. He saw that one of the warriors was distinguished by the most magnificent war-gear. His massive sword was damascened with a wavy serpent pattern. His shield was inlaid with the wild beasts of battle. And at his side lay a flashing crown.

"You see?" said Loomis.

"Yes," breathed Owen. "King Arthur! Arthur's warriors!" He saw two great heaps in the middle of the circle — one heap of gold coins, one of silver.

"You can take that away," said Loomis. "As much as you can carry."

"The gold and silver?" said Owen.

"Not both," said Loomis. "One or the other. They won't wake."

Owen picked his way down the steps and softly past the sleeping heads and into the circle. He filled his pockets with gold, his shoes with gold, he opened his shirt and stuffed gold into it.

"And you?" said Owen, when he had got back to the steps.

Loomis shook his head.

"Why not?" asked Owen.

"What's the use of it?" said Loomis.

With that, he led the way out of the cavern. Clinking and clanking, Owen followed him.

"Watch the bell!" said Loomis. "If you touch it, one of the warriors will wake. He'll lift his head," said Loomis, "and ask, 'Is it the day?' And you must call out at once, 'No! Not yet! Sleep on!'"

"And then?" Owen whispered.

"And then he'll lay down his head again and go back to sleep."

Owen was so heavy with gold that, while he was trying to edge round the bell, he staggered and banged into it. The clapper swung: the bell rang. At once a sleeping warrior raised his head and called out, "Is it the day?"

"No!" shouted Owen. "Not yet! Sleep on!"

So Owen and Loomis got out of the cave, and levered the flat stone back over the entrance, and replanted the hazel tree.

"You'll be going up the road now to your parents," said Loomis. "And I'm going to walk down out of the mountains."

Owen looked at Loomis — his kind and curiously blank face, his bright blue eyes.

"No point in asking," said Loomis. "Just learn to look."

"Yes," said Owen.

"You've enough gold there to last for years."

"Yes," said Owen again.

"And you can always go back down. You know the way down and you can take some more: gold or silver, one or the other. But be careful of that bell."

"No!" said Owen quickly. "Not yet! Sleep on!"

"That's it," said Loomis.

"And King Arthur?" asked Owen. "And his sleeping warriors?"

"Sleeping and ready," Loomis replied, "ready for the day when the Black Eagle and the Golden Eagle go to war. When they fight, the ground will tremble; then the bell will ring and the warriors will wake. Those warriors, they'll fight all the enemies of Wales, and conquer the whole Island of Britain."

"I know a song about that," said Owen.

"The Welsh will rise: they will give battle . . .
war-bands round the ale and soldiers in swarms . . .
Every Welshman's son will shout for joy . . ."

Loomis looked rather pleased. "The Welsh," he said, drawing himself up to his full height, such as it was, and raising one hand, "will have their king and government at Caerleon, as they used to do. Wales will be a country of justice and peace for as long as this world lasts."

Owen did not use the gold wisely or well. True, he did set up his parents in a new house, but that was all he had to show for it. He left his job in stinking London; he never did another day's work; he gambled; and within five years he had very little gold left.

Owen returned alone to the cavern. He entered it and gazed on sleeping Arthur and his warriors, and once again reeled out under the weight of a great load of gold. On his way back down the passage, Owen bumped into the bell. The bell rang and a warrior lifted his head.

"Is it the day?" he called, and his voice echoed round and round the cavern.

Owen was out of breath. And he was scared — so scared that the words froze in his head. He knew they were in there and he couldn't remember them.

Several warriors woke now. They came out from the cavern into the gloomy passageway. They took hold of Owen and shook him until the ground around him was carpeted in gold.

Then the warriors turned their lances and beat squealing Owen with the wooden shafts. They thrashed him and broke his arms and ribs and legs. Then they threw him out of the passageway on to the soft soil above, and drew the flat stone back over the entrance.

Owen crawled through the wood, past the pool where the rivers Mellte and Sychryd meet, and down to the little road. There his own parents found him. And in the high village where he had been born, he lived poor and crippled for the rest of his life.

Quite often Owen returned with friends to the oak- and ash- and hazel-wood under the soaring dark rock. They looked for the entrance to the cavern. They dug for it. How they dug for it. It was there and it was not there.

BILLY

Billy wasn't born a cripple. He fell out of the apple tree when he was four and broke both his legs. He broke them in several places.

There was no doctor within a day's ride of the village, so the two wise women laid poor Billy on a table, and prepared splints, and set his legs as best they could. The legs set crooked, though, very crooked, and from that day forward Billy was unable to walk.

While his friends played chase and turned cartwheels, and flexed their lengthening limbs, all Billy could do was haul himself along on a pair of blackthorn sticks. Everyone liked him though. They had no end of time for him because he was cheerful and brave, and made the most of his life. His friends always carted him round to their games and gatherings.

When he grew up, Billy became a tailor. The little cripple sat cross-legged in his cottage surrounded by bright rings of talk and laughter. And after supper, he used to swing along on his sticks in the direction of the village pub.

One Hallowe'en, while Billy and his friends were sitting in the pub, a band of guisers burst in with howls and shouts. The boys wore girls' clothing, the girls wore shirts and trousers, and all their faces were blackened with soot. At once they blew out the publican's two paraffin lamps, which stood at each end of the bar, and then they swung their own turnip lanterns in front of the drinkers.

Billy and his friends stared at the swinging faces—their fiery eyes and rough-cut mouths, their glow and flicker. And later, when the guisers had been given food and drink and gone on their way, leaving behind them an aftertow of quiet and emptiness, the publican said: "That's scared off the ghosts, then."

A log hissed and spat in the grate.

"There'll be ghosts in the churchyard, though," said a voice.

"That's no place to be tonight," another voice exclaimed.

"I'm not frit!" said Billy quickly.

"The churchyard," said the publican. "That's alive tonight . . ."

"I'm not frit," said Billy again. "I'll go to the churchyard. I'll sit and sew there all night."

Laughing and alert, Billy's friends carried him back to his cottage to collect cloth and needle and thread; then they took one of the farmer's carts and rolled the cripple up the hill to the graveyard.

"Come on, Billy!" said a voice.

"See you in the morning, Billy," said several voices.

In the moonlight the tailor sat down on a flagstone, and spread out his cloth. It was so bright that he could see to sew. Billy sewed until eleven o'clock, and sewed until twelve o'clock . . .

Then Billy heard a rumble of a voice from the headstone right behind him. The grave began to open and Billy was showered with fistfuls of sand. Out came a head and the head thundered, "Do you see this head without flesh or blood?"

"Yes," said the tailor, "I see that, but I sew this."

"Do you see this arm without flesh or blood?"

"Yes," said the tailor, "I see that, but I sew this."

"Do you see this body without flesh or blood?"

"Yes," said the tailor, "I see that, but I sew this."

By now a huge man, eight foot tall, had come out of the grave. As he started to speak again, Billy finished his piece of sewing; he raised the cloth to his mouth and bit off the thread.

Then the thing reached out and clawed at Billy with its huge bone-hand.

The little tailor leaped up. He pelted across the churchyard and jumped right over the wall.

"Do you see this? Do you see this?" shouted the tailor. And he ran all the way home, laughing.

MOSSYCOAT

There was once a poor old widow who lived in a little cottage. She had one daughter who was nineteen and very beautiful. Day after day her mother busied herself spinning a coat for her.

A pedlar came courting this girl. He called at the cottage regularly, and kept bringing her this trinket and that trinket. He was in love with her, and badly wanted her to marry him.

But the girl wasn't in love with him; things didn't work out as easily as that. She didn't know quite what to do for the best, and asked her mother for advice.

"Let him come," said her mother. "Get what you can out of him while I finish this coat. After that, you won't need him or his pretty little presents. You tell him, girl," the mother said, "that you won't marry him unless he gets you a white satin dress embroidered with sprigs of gold as big as a man's hand; and mind you tell him it must be a perfect fit."

Next time the pedlar came round, and asked the daughter to marry him, she told him just this — the very same words her mother had used.

The pedlar looked at the girl, and took stock of her size and build. And within a week, he was back with the dress. It was made of white satin and embroidered with sprigs of gold, and when the girl went upstairs with her mother and tried it on, it was a perfect fit.

"What shall I do now, mother?" asked the girl.

"Tell him," said her mother, "that you won't marry him unless he gets you a dress made of silk the colour of all the birds of the air. And it must be a perfect fit."

The girl told the pedlar just this, and in two or three days he was back at the cottage with the coloured silk dress. And since he knew her size from the first dress, of course it was a perfect fit.

"Now what shall I do?" asked the girl.

"Tell him," said her mother, "that you won't marry him unless he gets you a pair of silver slippers that are a perfect fit."

The girl told the pedlar just this, and in a few days he called round with them. The girl's feet were only about three inches long, but the slippers were a perfect fit. They were not too tight; neither were they too loose.

Once more the girl asked her mother what she should do.

"I can finish the coat tonight," said her mother, "and then you won't need the pedlar. Tell him," she said, "that you'll marry him tomorrow. Tell him to be here at ten o'clock."

The girl told the pedlar just this. "Ten o'clock in the morning," she said.

"I'll be there, my love," said the pedlar. "By heaven, I will!"

That night the girl's mother worked on the coat until very late, but she finished it all right. Green moss and gold thread, that's what it was made of: just those two things. "Mossycoat", the woman called it; and that's what she called the daughter she had made it for.

"It's a magic coat," she said. "A wishing coat! When you've got it on, you have only to wish to be somewhere, and you'll be there that very instant. And you've only to wish if you want to change yourself into something else, like a swan, or a bee."

Next morning the widow was up at dawn. She called her daughter, and told her that it was time for her to go out into the world and seek her fortune. "And a handsome fortune it must be," she said.

"What about the pedlar?" asked the girl.

"I'll send him packing when he comes round," said her mother. "Don't give him another thought."

The old widow was a seer and knew what was going to happen. She gave her daughter the mossycoat and a gold crown. "Take the two dresses and silver slippers as well," she said. "But travel in your working clothes."

So Mossycoat was ready to set off, and she put on her coat of green moss and gold thread.

"Wish yourself a hundred miles away," her mother said. "Then keep walking until you come to a big hall, and ask for a job there. You won't have far to walk, my blessed. They're bound to find you work at the big hall."

Mossycoat did as her mother told her, and soon she found herself in front of a big house belonging to a gentleman. She knocked at the front door and said she was looking for work. Well, the long and the short of it was that the mistress of the house herself came down to see her; and her ladyship liked the look of her.

"What work can you do?" she asked.

"I can cook, your ladyship," said Mossycoat. "In fact, people say I'm a very good cook."

"I can't employ you as cook," the lady said. "I've got one already. But I'll engage you to help the cook, if that will satisfy you."

"Thank you, your ladyship," said Mossycoat. "I'll be really happy in this house."

So it was settled that Mossycoat was to be the undercook. And after her ladyship had showed her up to her bedroom, she took her down to the kitchen and introduced her to the other servants.

"This is Mossycoat," she told them, "and I've engaged her," she said, "to be the undercook."

Then the mistress of the house left them, and Mossycoat went up to her bedroom again, to unpack her belongings, and hide away her gold crown and silver slippers, and her silk and satin dresses.

The other kitchen girls were beside themselves with jealousy; and it didn't help matters that the new girl was far more beautiful than any of them.

"Here's this vagrant in rags," one girl said, "and she's put above us."

"All she's fit for," said another, "is work in the scullery."

"Undercook!" cried a third girl. "If anyone's going to be undercook, it should be one of us."

"One of us," said the fourth girl. "Not a girl in rags and tatters picked up off the street."

"We'll put her in her place!" the girls said. "That we will!"

So they went on and on until Mossycoat came down again, ready to start work. Then they really set about her.

"Who on earth do you think you are, setting yourself above us?"

"You're going to be the undercook, are you?"

"No fear!"

"What you're going to do is scour the pans."

"And polish the knives."

"And clean the grates."

"And that's all you're good for."

Then down came the milk-skimmer on the top of her head, pop, pop, pop.

"That's what you deserve," they told her. "And, my lady, that's what you'll get."

So that is how things were for Mossycoat. She was given all the dirtiest work, and soon she was up to her ears in grease, and her face was as black as soot. And every now and again one or another of the servants would pop, pop, pop her on top of the head with the skimmer, until Mossycoat's head was so sore she could scarcely stand it.

Days turned into weeks, weeks into months and Mossycoat was still scouring the pans and polishing the knives and cleaning the grate; and the servants were still pop, pop, popping her on the head with the skimmer.

Now there was going to be a big dance in a grand house nearby. It was to last three nights, with hunting and other sports during the daytime. All the gentry from miles around were going to be there; and of course the master and mistress and their son—they only had one child—planned to be there.

This dance was all the talk among the servants.

"I wish I could go," said one girl.

"I'd like to dance with some of those young gentlemen," said a second.

"I'd like to see what dresses the ladies wear," said a third.

And so they all went on — all except Mossycoat.

"If only we'd the clothes," said one, "we'd be all right. We're just as good as their ladyships any day."

"And you, Mossycoat," said another. "Wouldn't you like to go?"

"You'd look just right in all your rags and dirt," they said.

And down came the skimmer on Mossycoat's head, pop, pop, pop. Then they all laughed at her. What crude people they were!

Now Mossycoat was very handsome, and no amount of rags and dirt could hide the fact. The other servants might think as they liked, but the young master had his eye on Mossycoat, and the master and mistress had always taken particular notice of her, because of her fine looks.

On the first day of the big dance, they sent for her and asked her if she would like to come with them.

"Thank you," said Mossycoat, "but I'd never dream of such a thing. I know my place better than that. Besides," she said, "I'd cover one side of the coach with grease. And I'd sully the clothes of anyone I danced with."

The master and mistress made light of that, but no matter what they said, they were unable to change Mossycoat's mind.

When Mossycoat got back to the kitchen, she told the other servants why she had been sent for.

"What! You?" exclaimed one servant. "I don't believe it!"

"If it had been one of us, that would have been different."

"You'd grease all the gentlemen's clothes — if there are

any who would dance with a scullery girl."

"And the ladies, they'd be forced to hold their noses when they walked past you."

"No," they said, "we don't believe the master and mistress ever asked you to go to the ball with them. You must be lying," they said.

And down came the skimmer on top of her head, pop, pop, pop.

On the next evening, the master and the mistress, and their son too, asked Mossycoat to go to the dance.

"It was a grand affair last night," said the master.

"And it'll be even grander this evening," added the mistress.

"Do come with us," said their son. "Mossycoat, I beg you."

But Mossycoat said no. She said she couldn't go on account of her rags and her grease and her dirt. Even the young master was unable to persuade her, and it wasn't for want of trying.

The other servants refused to believe Mossycoat when she told them that she had been invited again to the dance, and added that the young master had been very pressing.

"Listen to her!" they cried. "What next? What an upstart! And all lies!" they said.

Then one of the servants snorted and grabbed the skimmer and down it came once again, pop, pop, pop, on Mossycoat's head.

That night, Mossycoat decided to go to the dance, all dressed up, and all on her own, without anybody knowing about it.

The first thing she did was to put all the other servants under a spell. As she moved around, she just touched each of them, without being noticed, and each fell asleep as soon as she did so.

Next, Mossycoat had a really good wash, her first since she had come to the big house. She had never been allowed to before. The other servants had made her dirty and kept her dirty.

Then Mossycoat went up to her bedroom. She threw off her working clothes and shoes, and put on her white satin dress embroidered with gold sprigs, her silver slippers, and her gold crown. And, of course, underneath the dress, she was wearing the mossycoat.

When she was ready, Mossycoat just wished herself at the dance; and as soon as she had spoken, there she was! She did just feel herself soaring up and flying through the air, but only for a moment. Then she was standing in the ballroom.

The young master noticed Mossycoat standing on her own, and once he had seen her, he was unable to take his eyes off her. He had never seen anyone so handsome, nor so beautifully dressed, in his life.

"Who is she?" the young man asked his mother.

"I don't know," said the mistress. "I've never seen her before."

"Can't you find out, mother?" he said. "Can't you go and talk to her?"

The young man's mother saw he would never rest until she did, so she walked up and introduced herself to the young lady, and asked her who she was, and where she came from, and so on. But all she could get out of her was that she came from a place where they hit her on the head with a skimmer.

After a while, the young master went over and introduced himself, but Mossycoat didn't tell him her name; she gave nothing away.

"Well, will you dance with me?" asked the young master.

"Thank you," said Mossycoat, "but I'd rather not."

But the young man stayed at Mossycoat's side. He kept asking her to dance, over and over again.

"All right!" said Mossycoat. "Just once."

The young man and Mossycoat danced once, up the length of the ballroom and back down again; and then Mossycoat said she had to leave. The young man pressed her to stay, but it was a waste of breath; she was determined to go, there and then.

"All right," said the young man. "I'll come and see you off."

But Mossycoat just wished she were back in the big house, and there she was! So the young master wasn't able to see her off! She vanished from his side in the twinkling of an eye, leaving him there gaping in astonishment.

Thinking she might be out in the entrance hall, or in the porch, waiting for her carriage, the young man went out to look for her; but there was no sign of her anywhere, inside or out, and no one he asked had seen her leave. The young man went back to the ballroom, but he was unable to think of anything or anyone but the mysterious girl, and took no further interest in the ball.

When Mossycoat got back to the big house, she made sure that all the other servants were still under her spell. Then she went up to her bedroom and changed into her working clothes; and when she had done that, she came down to the kitchen again and touched each of the servants.

That broke the spell and woke them. One by one they started up, wondering what time of day it was, and how long they had been asleep.

"A long time!" said Mossycoat. "The whole evening, in fact! The mistress wouldn't like to know about this, would she?"

The servants begged Mossycoat not to let on, and offered her bribes to keep quiet about it. They gave her a skirt, a pair of shoes, a pair of stockings, some stays; they were all old enough but they still had a bit of wear in them. So Mossycoat promised to say nothing about it.

And that night, they didn't hit her over the head with the skimmer.

All next day the young master was restless. He could think of nothing but the young lady he had seen the night before and fallen in love with at first sight. He kept wondering whether she would be at the dance again that evening, and how he could stop her from disappearing.

I must find out where she lives, he thought. *Otherwise, how will I be able to bear it when the dance is over?*

"I'll die," the young man told his mother, "if I'm not able to marry her." He was madly in love with her!

"Well," said his mother, "she seemed a nice, modest girl. But she wouldn't say who she was or who her family are. She wouldn't say where she came from, except that it was a place where they hit her on the head with a skimmer!"

"She's a mystery, I know," said the young man, "but that doesn't mean I want her any the less. I must marry her, mother," he said, "whoever she is and whatever she is. That's God's truth, mother, and strike me dead if it isn't!"

It wasn't long before the young master and this wonderful, handsome lady he had fallen in love with were all the talk in the kitchen.

"And fancy you, Mossycoat, thinking he especially

wanted you to go to the dance," they said. And then they really set about her, making all kinds of sarcastic remarks, and hitting her on the head with the skimmer, pop, pop, pop, for lying to them.

It was just the same later on, too, when Mossycoat returned to the kitchen after declining to go to the dance for the third time. "This is your last chance," said the servants. "You're such a liar, Mossycoat! We'll give you one more chance." And down came the skimmer on the top of her head, pop, pop, pop.

Then Mossycoat put the whole devil's breed of them under a spell just as she had done the night before, and got herself ready to go to the dance. The only difference was that this time she put on her other dress — the dress made of silk the colour of all the birds of the air. And underneath the dress, she was wearing the mossycoat, of course.

When Mossycoat entered the ballroom, the young master was watching and waiting for her. His horse was ready saddled and standing at the door. He went over to the young lady and asked her for a dance.

She said just the same as on the night before: no at first, and in the end, yes. And as soon as they had danced up the length of the ballroom and back down again, she said she had to leave. This time, however, the young man kept his arm round the girl's waist until they got outside.

But then Mossycoat wished she were back in the big house, and almost as soon as she had spoken, she was there! The young man felt her rise into the air but he was unable to do anything about it. Maybe he did just touch her foot, though, because she dropped one slipper.

The young man picked up the slipper. But as for catching up with the girl, it would have been easier to catch up with the wind on a stormy night.

As soon as she got home, Mossycoat changed back into her old clothes. Then she released the servants from the spell. When they realised that they had fallen asleep again, one offered her a shilling and another half-a-crown — a third of a week's wages — not to let on; and once again Mossycoat promised to keep quiet about it.

The young master spent the next day in bed, dying for the love of the young lady who had dropped one of her silver slippers on the previous night. The doctors were unable to do anything for him at all, so the young man's parents decided to make his condition known. They said the only person able to save his life was the young lady whose foot fitted the silver slipper — and that the slipper was only about three inches long. They promised that if she would come forward, the young master would marry her.

Ladies came from near and far, some with big feet and some with small, but none small enough for the silver slipper, however much they pinched and squeezed. Poor women came too, but it was just the same for them. And of course, all the servants tried on the slipper, but that was out of the question altogether.

All this time, the young master lay dying.

"Is there no one else?" asked his mother. "No one else at all? No rich lady? No poor woman?"

"No one," they said. "No one at all. Everyone has tried it on except for Mossycoat."

"Tell her to come here at once," said the mistress.

So the other servants fetched Mossycoat.

"Mossycoat!" said the mistress. "Try this slipper on."

Mossycoat slipped her foot into it easily enough; it was a perfect fit. Then the young master jumped out of bed and opened his arms . . .

"Wait!" said Mossycoat, and she ran out of the room. Before long, though, she was back again wearing her satin dress with gold sprigs, her gold crown and both her silver slippers. Again the young master opened his arms . . .

"Wait!" said Mossycoat, and again she ran out of the room. This time she came back wearing her silk dress the colour of all the birds of the air. Mossycoat didn't stop the young master this time, and he took her into his arms and kissed her.

After all this, when at last the master and the mistress and the young man and Mossycoat had time to talk to one another quietly, there were one or two questions they wanted to ask her.

"How did you get to the dance and back again in no time?" they said.

"Just wishing," said Mossycoat. And she told them about the magic coat her mother had made for her, and the powers it gave her when she cared to use them.

"That explains everything!" said the mistress.

"But what did you mean," asked the master, "when you said you came from a place where they hit you on the head with a skimmer?"

"I meant just what I said," replied Mossycoat. "The skimmer's always coming down on my head, pop, pop, pop!"

The master and mistress were furious when they heard that. All the kitchen servants were told to leave and the dogs were sent after them to drive them right away from the place.

Then Mossycoat sent for her old mother and the master and mistress made her welcome at the big house. Mossycoat and the young master got married on the first day possible, and Mossycoat had a coach-and-six to ride in; she could have had a coach-and-ten if she had wanted, for as you can imagine her every wish was granted. The young man and Mossycoat were always happy together. Mossycoat's mother lived with them, and they had a basketful of children.

THE SHEPHERD'S TALE

That's where I saw them! Up on that green patch there . . .

That's fifty years, see. I was missing one ewe and high up and calling. First there was such a winking and glittering. Then I saw them quite clearly — little men and women dancing in a ring.

I'll tell you then. I hurried towards them and first thing caught my eye — they were wearing scarlet or white, every one of them. Scarlet or white. A kind of uniform, see. The men had tripled caps on their heads and the women, they wore white lacy kinds of things. Fantastical! They waved in the wind.

My! Those ladies were lovely! I've seen some beauties, mind, some rare beauties. The men, too, they were handsome.

There were three harpists there, sitting on flat stones and playing for the dancers. Plucking and rippling! The strange thing is I couldn't hear a note. I saw them playing but they didn't make a sound.

Round and round whirled the dancers, smiling and laughing. And when they spied me, they nodded and smiled, and some of them threw up their arms and beckoned me. Then they all joined hands again. Faster and faster, leaning backward, almost falling! Laughing faces!

There were others, too, mind. Little men running races, sprinting and scurrying, and others clambering over the old cromlech — up one side, along the top, and down the other. That's as old as Adam, that. Prehistorical! Not so long back, two men came all the way from Cardiff just to measure it . . .

Where was I then? Yes, and horses. There were ladies riding round on dapper white horses. Side-saddle, mind. Nothing wanton! Their dresses were white — white as misty sunlight and red as young blood.

Well, then, I'll tell you. I came close and very close. I stuck out one foot, just into the ring. I heard it then, the fairy music. Harps, what a sound, yes! My heart started jigging. There's a sound a man could die for.

So I stepped right into the ring, see. At once I saw I was in some kind of palace. The walls were covered with gold and pearls.

One young woman walked up to me. "Come with me, Dai!" That's what she said. "We've been expecting you."

Then she showed me round — all the shining rooms, and the coloured gardens.

"You can go where you want, Dai," she said. "There's just one thing . . ."

"What's that?" I said.

"You see this well?"

I looked into the well and it was teeming with fish, see. Red and blue and black and green. And some of them were gold.

"You see this well?" she said. "Whatever you do, Dai, never drink a drop."

The young woman led me back through the palace to a feasting-hall. There was venison and lamb and sucking-pig; pheasant and grouse and pigeon. All of it carried in on silver platters, mind. And you know who carried it? Beautiful ladies! That was a place, all right!

And there was red wine and yellow wine, I remember that. I drank them both, see. I drank them from gold goblets covered with diamonds and rubies and emeralds. Strong wine and sweet wine! Before then, I'd only tasted water and milk and beer.

Whatever I wanted, they brought it to me. Food, drink, warm water to wash with, a comfortable bed. I wanted harpists, singers, acrobats! Then I wanted to talk to their little children. A whole troop came in, chattering and giggling. They were small as dandelions.

You know what I wanted most? It's always the same, mind. You want what you can't have. That's the old Adam.

After dark, I sneaked out into the garden, see. I ran down to the well. Then I plunged in this hand — and all the coloured fishes, they disappeared. Then I cupped my hands and lowered them into the water . . .

Oh! What a shriek there was! Glassy and piercing, like the moon in pain. A shriek right round the garden and the palace.

Never mind, I closed my eyes and sipped the water!

The garden and the palace and the little people inside it, they all dissolved. In front of my eyes they just dissolved. Mountain mist.

It was dark, hopeless dark, and I was standing alone on the side of the mountain. Up there, that green patch, see. Standing right in the place where I stepped into the ring.

THE COW THAT ATE THE PIPER

The three hired men left the farm on a cold November morning. They slung their sacks over their shoulders and set out on the long walk back home to Kerry.

That evening, the moon shone and the north wind pursed his blue lips and whistled. And the three men couldn't see so much as a haystack, let alone an old barn, to shelter and sleep in. They quickened their pace, they trotted, they sang, they swung their arms, and before long they fell into step with a laughing piper. He was barefooted and wearing no more than a tatter of clothing.

"I'll go along with you," said the piper.

The frost tightened his white fist: bushes by the roadside hunched their shoulders; the road began to glitter.

"We're all dead men," said the piper, "if we don't keep moving."

The four of them kept walking, trotting, walking and shortly before midnight, they came across a dead man lying right across the road. He was wearing a brand-new pair of shoes.

"Faith!" said the piper. "Look at those shoes!"

The three men looked and the moon polished the shining toecaps.

"And I haven't so much as a stitch on my feet," said the piper. "They're no use to him, are they now?"

"Not at all!" said one of the hired men.

"I'll take them off of him," said the piper. He got down on all fours and tugged at the dead man's shoes. But he could do no more than untie the laces.

"Death alive!" exclaimed the piper. "They're frozen to his feet!"

"Come on now," said another of the hired labourers. "We're decent men."

"Give me your spade!" the piper said. "Let's see if I can't cut off his legs."

So the piper cut off the dead man's feet at the ankles. He picked them up and popped them into his sack. Then he and the hired men hurried on and just after midnight, they came upon a little farm.

"Heaven be praised!" said the piper.

The men knocked, they waited, knocked again and after rather a long time a sleepy serving-girl unbolted the door and let them into the kitchen—a low-slung smoky room with the fire at one end and three cows tied up at the other.

"You can sleep here," said the girl. "But keep clear of that grey cow. She's a devil. She'll eat the coats off of your backs." The girl latched the door at the foot of the stairs, and padded up to her own room.

Before long, the three hired men curled up round the burning peats and fell asleep. The piper, though, still had work to do. He opened his sack and took out the shoes with the two feet inside them, and toasted them over the fire. The feet began to thaw and he was soon able to pull off the shoes.

The piper smiled. He drummed his fingers on the shining toecaps and hummed a little tune. Then he put his own feet into the shoes! He stood up; he hopped and spun around; and he threw the dead man's feet down the far end of the kitchen.

For a while the piper dozed. Then at dawn, while the household and the hired men were still asleep, he got up, shouldered his pipes and his sack, and crept out of the house.

The serving-girl was first to rise. She came downstairs, and roused the huddle of sleepers. The three hired men groaned and rubbed their eyes and sat up.

"There were four of you at midnight," said the girl.

The men yawned and ran their hands through their hair.

"Where's the one with the pipes?"

"I don't know," said the first man.

"How should we know?" said the second man. And the third man just shrugged. The girl walked down to the far end of the kitchen and there she stumbled right over the two feet.

"Holy mother!" she cried. "The cow has eaten him!"

The serving-girl ran to the foot of the staircase. "The cow!" she yelled. "The grey cow! The cow has eaten the piper!"

"What's that?" shouted the farmer, and he stumped down the stairs, a great rumple-and-crease of a man.

"The cow's eaten the piper!" shouted the girl. "The poor cold piper! There's only his feet left."

The big pink farmer looked at the feet. He looked at the

hired men and the men advanced to the middle of the room.

"There were four last night then," he said.

"There were," said the first man.

"And our comrade," said the second, "he's been eaten by that grey cow."

The farmer looked round him, as if the walls themselves had ears. "Shush!" he said, and he put a stubby finger to his lips. "No need for any trouble now."

Then the farmer dipped into his clothing and fished out five gold coins. "Here's five guineas for you," he said, pressing the coins into the palm of the first hired man. "Now eat your breakfast and be off."

As soon as they had eaten breakfast, and it was not a small one, the three hired men shouldered their sacks and left the little farm.

Some way down the winding road, they caught up with a laughing man wearing no more than a tatter of clothing. The golden sun polished his toecaps and he was hopping and spinning and dancing a jig.

THE GREEN CHILDREN

Clac straightened his back, braced his aching shoulders, and grunted. Sweat trickled down his face and dripped from the end of his nose. He licked his lips; they tasted of salt. Clac glanced down the long, straight swaths of corn; then, rubbing the back of his neck between his shoulder blades, he considered the position of the sun. But his stomach was his best clock. He filled his lungs, cupped a huge hand to his mouth, and bellowed "Food".

The other cottars heard him. One by one they stopped work and mopped their brows; one by one they left their own strips of land and began to walk slowly towards him.

Their scythes gleamed in the midday sun; a very small wind moved over the swaths and whispered warnings to the ears of uncut corn.

"Come on," called Clac. He sat on the turf ridge dividing his strip from the next, waiting impatiently. "This sun . . . I've had enough of it."

"So have I," sighed Swein, collapsing in a heap like a sack of potatoes.

"Come on," cried Clac, "you and you and all the rest of you." He picked up a flitch of bacon with one hand and with the other a leather bottle of cider. "I'm for the shade. Shade first, then food. Who'll carry the apples?"

"I will," said Grim.

So the cottars, nine of them in all, set off across the common land, on which their cattle grazed. They walked towards the Wolfpits—where, in winter, wild creatures roamed—and towards the high, waving elms.

Clac led the way. He always did; he liked leading. And the lord of the manor, Sir Richard de Calne, who had recognised this quality in him, had put him over the other cottars and villeins. As the tired, hungry men approached the elms, Clac stopped in his tracks. "Look!"

"What?" said Grim.

"Where?" said Swein.

"Look!" Clac exclaimed again. "Look! There!" He pointed towards the trees. "Follow me." And throwing down the flitch and the bottle, he started to run. He ran and ran until at last he came to the old Wolfpits just beyond the elms.

And there, huddling in the hollow of the largest pit, the cottars saw what Clac had seen: two green children. Their skin was green, their hair was green, they wore green clothes. And one was a boy and the other was a girl.

For a moment, nobody moved, nobody spoke. The cottars looked down at the green children and the green children looked up at the cottars.

"Blessed Edmund preserve us!" exclaimed Clac. And he made the sign of the cross.

"And St. William of Norwich," muttered Grim. And he crossed himself too.

"Who can they be?" said Swein.

"Ask them," said Clac.

Swein laughed nervously.

"All right then," said Clac. "I will. I'll ask them." But he was nervous too; the break in his voice betrayed him.

The cottars bunched together anxiously.

"They may be little folk," Swein warned him.

"Let's leave them alone," said Thurketil.

"Look at them," Clac replied. "Do they look as if they mean harm?"

The cottars crowded round the edge of the pit, watching breathlessly. If one man had moved, the rest would have toppled headlong down. The boy and the girl were clutching one another, looking up at the nine men fearfully. And then, quite unexpectedly, the green girl buried her face in her hands and began to sob.

"You see?" said Clac. He stepped forward, slipped down the grassy bank, and walked towards the children.

When Clac came closer to the children, he was so astonished that he completely forgot his nervousness. In all his thirty years, he had never seen or even heard of anything like it before: green children . . . a boy and a girl with green cheeks, green fingers, and, poking out of their green sandals, green toes.

"Hallo!" said Clac in his gruff, friendly voice. "Who are you?"

The children huddled still closer together. They gazed at Clac, bewildered.

Clac looked at the children closely, and thought the girl was about nine and the boy about seven. He saw they resembled each other not only because they were green, but also in the mould of their features. "You must be brother and sister," he said. "Who are you? Where do you come from?"

The children continued to gaze at him silently.

"Well," thought Clac, "either they're dumb or they don't understand me."

At this moment the boy turned to the girl and spoke several strange words.

"That settles it," said Clac. "You don't understand me . . . And I can't pretend to understand you."

The green girl looked at Clac; suddenly, she flashed a smile at him, opened her mouth and pointed at it.

"Blessed Edmund preserve me!" exclaimed Clac. "She's got a green tongue." He nodded and grinned. "I see," he said. "You're hungry."

He turned round, waved reassuringly to the other cottars, and called, "What are you doing up there, you idlers? Get the flitch and bring it down. And bring the cider too."

In no time, the cottars were pouring down into the pit, bringing the food with them. They swarmed round the children, their superstition at last overcome by curiosity.

"Here! Give me the flitch," said Clac. He took it from Swein, then showed it to the two children. They looked at it blankly, then turned to each other and shook their heads. Then the girl sniffed it, and wrinkled up her nose.

"Look at that!" marvelled Clac. "They've never seen a flitch before."

Now it was his turn to shake his head.

"What about the apples, then?" he said. "Give me two red apples."

"Here," said Grim, and passed them over. The two

children looked at them, turned to each other again, and shook their heads a second time.

Clac was dumbfounded. "What do you think of that?" he said. "They've never seen apples before."

Despite their behaviour, it was clear that the two children were famished. Again and again they pointed to their mouths. And once more the green girl began to weep.

"I think we should take them to Sir Richard," said Clac. "Sir Richard's a traveller. He's travelled far and wide, almost as far as the edges of the earth. Perhaps he's heard of green children."

So the cottars escorted the green children to the manor of Sir Richard de Calne. And as they walked, they sang, for they were not altogether sorry to miss an afternoon's work under the blazing sun. But the children were dazzled by the bright light. They kept their heads down, and shielded their eyes with their arms.

The fortified manor was surrounded by a moat. Clac strode to the brink, and shouted to the guards on the other side. For a while the guards conferred, then they let the drawbridge down. The little group, with the children in their midst, walked across and on into the great hall.

"Wait here!" said a guard, his eyes bulging out of his head as he looked at the two children. "Until Sir Richard comes."

Inside the hall, out of the sunlight, the children looked about them with great curiosity. They ran to and fro, exclaiming in wonder at the huge stone fireplace, the narrow windowslits, the yellow rushes on the floor. They chattered excitedly, and for a moment even forgot their hunger.

"Green children," boomed a voice at the entrance of the

hall. "What's all this?" And there, hands on hips, stood Sir Richard de Calne, an enormous, pot-bellied man.

The cottars liked him well. He was a just lord, and a generous one, though his moods were as variable as the weather.

But now he was completely silent. He was staring at the green children open-mouthed.

"Please, my lord," said Clac, stepping forward. And he explained to Sir Richard how he had discovered the green children at the Wolfpits.

"And they don't speak English," he said, "and they won't eat our food."

From his great height, Sir Richard looked down at the shrinking children. He stroked his beard and considered the problem: green children, green as grass, who couldn't speak English, who wouldn't eat apples . . .

"So they don't speak English," echoed Sir Richard after a long pause. "Ah well! Perhaps they speak Norman." He stooped, smiled warmly at the green girl, and began, "D'où venez-vous?"

The green girl looked to her brother, and he repeated the strange words that Clac had heard in the Wolfpits. Then the girl looked up at Sir Richard, pointed at his pot-belly and opened her mouth.

Sir Richard bellowed with laughter. "I understand you," he cried. "Food's a common language. All right. Sit them down." Then, walking to the entrance of the hall, he shouted at the top of his voice, "Food! Food!"

Clac led the two children over to the trestle table and in no time, a servant bustled in, bearing a chicken on a platter; a second followed, carrying a bunch of grapes; and the third brought a pitcher of red wine.

"Give them each a wing," said Sir Richard. "That'll

tempt them. You see if it doesn't."

But the children pushed the chicken away.

"What about the grapes, then?" asked Sir Richard.

The black, succulent grapes were set before them. The girl fingered one and said something to her brother. Then they refused them too.

Sir Richard strode up and down the hall, disconcerted. "Bring them some cheese, then," he said.

Before long, a servant reappeared with a bowl of cream cheese, and placed that on the table. But the two children took one look at it and pushed that away too.

"Well!" exclaimed Sir Richard. "I don't know. What *will* they eat?"

It so happened that an old servant was crossing the far end of the hall. In his arms, he carried a pile of freshly cut beans, still attached to their stalks. Seeing the beans, the green children cried out with delight. They leaped up from the bench and ran towards the old man. He was so startled at the sight of them that he threw down the beans on the spot and ran out of the hall as fast as his old legs could carry him.

The children fell upon the pile and immediately began to tear open the stalks, thinking the beans were in the hollows of them. Finding none, they were utterly dismayed and began to weep dismally once more.

"Look!" said Clac. "Like this." He quickly opened a pod and showed them the naked beans.

And so at last the green children began to eat.

The cottars stood watching them.

"I see," said Sir Richard eventually. "I see. Green children, green food."

After they had eaten their fill, the green children smiled gratefully at Sir Richard de Calne and the cottars.

"Well!" said Sir Richard. "What are we going to do with them now?"

This was a question no one could answer. And as the two children showed no inclination to leave the hall, Sir Richard instructed that they should be allowed to remain at the manor for as long as they desired. He asked his priest, Father John, to teach them to speak English.

And for many, many months the green children ate nothing but beans.

The great fair at Stourbridge came and went. Sir Richard de Calne journeyed there, laden with packs of wool, and returned with Baltic furs, French cloth and lace, and salts and spices from the East. And all this time the green children stayed at the manor.

Father John took his duties seriously; each day the children had English lessons with him. They both worked hard and made good progress.

And the old priest, a lean, angular man who often declared he loved no one but God, began to love the green boy and the green girl as if they were his own children.

"They must be baptised," he told Sir Richard one day. "They may be green but they still have souls."

And so the children were baptised. The ceremony was attended by Sir Richard de Calne and by all his household, and by his cottars and villeins.

August grew old; September was born. High winds wrestled with the sun. Leaves fell, carpeting the earth in copper and bronze and gold. The elms by the Wolfpits looked like skeletons.

Clac and his fellow cottars brought the harvest home and began to prepare for winter. They killed pigs and cattle and fowls, and gave them to their wives who cut them up, and salted them, and stored them away for harder days.

During the cold days of November, the green boy became listless. He would eat no more beans; he made little progress in his work; he lost interest in playing draughts and spinning tops; and nothing his sister said could cheer him. Nobody could say what was wrong with him; he ran no fever, sported no spots. And his sister could speak so little English she was unable to explain.

Father John was anxious. He made the green boy eat mugwort and mayweed, crab-apple, thyme and fennel; he sent to Bury for water from the Well of Our Lady; he offered prayers.

It was all to no avail. One dark day, when the ground was like iron underfoot and the shifting skies were grey, the green boy threw up his hands and died.

Throughout the long hard winter his sister could not be consoled. Often she wept; it was so cold the tears froze on her cheeks. But at last, as spring threw off winter, she too threw off her grief. The crocuses flowered.

One evening Sir Richard de Calne and his family, his servants and guards, and all the cottars and villeins who worked on his demesne, gathered in the great hall.

After the meal it was customary for the minstrel to sing. The company turned from the tables to face the minstrel and the fire.

"Not tonight," called Sir Richard. "We'll not have songs tonight. I've asked you all for a special reason." He paused and looked round the hall. "Our guest," he continued, and smiling turned to the green girl, "can speak English at last. She has told me who she is, and where she comes from. And now I have asked her to tell her story to you."

There was a rustle of excitement.

The green girl stood up and walked over to the minstrel's place beside the flickering fire. Her shadow danced on the wall behind her. All at once she smiled, the same alluring smile she had first flashed at Clac in the Wolfpits. Then she began in a strong, clear voice, "I come from a green country. The people are green, the animals are green, the earth and sky are green. There is nothing that is not green.

"The sun never shines in my country. The light there is a constant green glow, as if the sun was always just below the horizon."

A puff of woodsmoke filled the room. The listeners coughed and rubbed their smarting eyes, then settled again. They had never heard such a thing in their lives.

"From the hills of our country," said the girl, "you can see another, much brighter land—though I have never been there—divided from ours by a broad river."

"But tell us where your land is," said Sir Richard, "and how you got here."

"Well! One day my brother and I—my poor brother who died of homesickness—we were tending sheep on the hills, and they began to stray. We followed them and came to the mouth of a cave, a great cave we'd never seen before. The sheep entered the cave and we walked in after them. And there, ahead of us, we heard the sound of bells: a most beautiful sound, loud bells and soft bells, treble bells and bass bells, ringing, ringing.

"It seemed," said the green girl, "that the sound came from the far end of the cave. The bells were so beautiful they pulled us towards them. We *had* to find them. So we walked through the cave, on and on. At first it was flat; then we began to climb. And the bells rang and rang, tugging us towards them.

"The cave was gloomy but not dark; then, suddenly, we saw a bright light some way ahead of us. 'That's where the bells are coming from,' my brother said. So we hurried towards it. It grew and grew, dazzling us. And all at once we climbed up and out, out of the cave," said the girl. "The ringing stopped, the sunlight blinded us." She clapped her hands to her eyes. "We were knocked senseless by the sun. We lay in a swoon for a long time . . ."

Everyone in the hall was leaning forward. The fire roared.

"When we recovered our senses, we saw we were in some deep pit. And although we looked for the entrance to the cave, it had completely gone; we couldn't find it again. 'What shall we do?' my brother asked me. 'I don't know,' I said. I felt rather afraid. 'But as we can't go back, we'd better go forward.' So, very cautiously, we climbed out of the Wolfpits . . ."

"That's it," exclaimed Clac excitedly. "I remember. That's when I saw you. 'Blessed Edmund preserve me,' I said. 'Two green children.'"

"If you were surprised to see green children," the girl replied, "think how astonished we were to see pink men!"

Everyone laughed.

"Not only astonished," continued the green girl, "but frightened too. My brother and I backed down into the pit again. But we couldn't find the entrance to the cave; and so you caught us."

The assembled company sighed, and nodded their heads.

"That's my story," said the green girl. "The rest you know. Thank you all for your great kindness to me. I've been very happy here; but if ever I can find the entrance to the cave, I must return home."

With that, she sat down.

But that was only the beginning. Many were the questions asked of her that night; many were the answers given.

The years passed and the green girl did not return home. She remained at the manor, for she was unable to find the entrance to the cave.

In time she learned to eat meat, and the fruits of the earth, and even to enjoy them. And slowly her skin lost its green tinge, her hair became fair.

She always said that she was very happy in this world. But often Clac and the cottars saw her wandering down by the Wolfpits, alone. At such times, they never went near her. For they knew that she must be lonely for her own people, and looking for the entrance to the cave.

One spring the green girl married. She left the manor of Sir Richard de Calne and went to live with her husband at Lenna near King's Lynn. But even then she used to return to the Wolfpits from time to time. Her feet were anchored to this earth, but her heart and mind sailed on to another far-off land.

How, then, did it end? What became of the girl who climbed up from the green land?

All this happened years and years ago. Eight hundred years ago. Some things live longer than centuries, others do not. We know much about the green girl, but there is much we do not know.

And nobody knows—unless you do—whether the green girl lived on earth to the end of her days; or whether, one day, near the Wolfpits, she simply disappeared.

THE FROG PRINCE

It was high and dry summer. The tall nettles behind the widow's cottage swayed and looked sorry for themselves. A silly warm wind chafed the elder leaves and the long grass.

The widow was making barley-cakes and realised she had too little water.

"We're out," she said to her daughter. "And I only need a thimbleful more."

"I'll go," said Jessie. "We'll be needing some later."

It was quite a walk through the hamlet and across the meadow, and when Jessie reached the well she found it was dry. There was not a drop of water in it.

Jessie sat down on the well's coping, feeling quite worn out. *I can't go back*, she thought, *not without some water. And there* is *no water* . . . Two tears slowly gathered in the corners of her eyes and, without knowing quite why, she began to weep.

Then a frog came leap-leap-leaping out of the well. He

hopped round the coping and looked up at Jessie. "What's wrong?" he said. "Lassie!" he said. "What are you crying for?"

"It's dry," sobbed Jessie. "There's no w-w-"

"Wipe your eyes!" said the frog. "If you'll marry me, I'll give you plenty of water."

Jessie wiped her eyes and smiled at the frog.

"You heard," said the frog.

Jessie didn't think the frog could be serious.

"Marry you!" she said. "Yes, of course I'll marry you!"

The frog took Jessie's earthenware jug and disappeared into the well. Two minutes later he was back and the jug was brimming with water.

Jessie shook her head and took the jug. "Thank you," she said. "Thank you very much."

The girl hurried home and her mother made the barley-cakes; and that night, just as they were about to go to bed, they heard something moving outside the door, and then they heard this song:

"Oh! open the door, my honey, my heart;
Open the door, my own true love.
Remember the promise you and I made
Down in the meadow, where we two met."

"What's that?" said the widow. "What's that song at the door?"

"Tut!" said Jessie, wrinkling up her pretty nose. "It's nothing but a filthy frog."

"Open the door for the poor frog," said the widow.

So Jessie opened the door and the frog came leap-leap-leaping in. He crossed the floor and sat down by the hearth. Then he sang:

"Oh! give me my supper, my honey, my heart;
Give me my supper, my own true love.
Remember the promise you and I made
Down in the meadow, where we two met."

"Tut!" said Jessie. "As if I would give supper to a filthy frog."

"Oh yes!" said the widow. "You must give the poor frog his supper."

So the frog got his supper and when he had finished it he sang again:

"Oh! take me to bed, my honey, my heart;
Take me to bed, my own true love.
Remember the promise you and I made
Down in the meadow, where we two met."

"Tut!" cried Jessie. "Would I ever take a filthy frog to bed?"

"Oh yes!" said the widow. "If that's what you promised, that's what you must do. Take the poor frog to bed."

So Jessie took the frog into her bed, and then he sang again:

"Now fetch me an axe, my honey, my heart;
Fetch me an axe, my own true love.
Remember the promise you and I made
Down in the meadow, where we two met."

Jessie went off to fetch an axe, and then the frog sang once more:

"Now chop off my head, my honey, my heart;
Chop off my head, my own true love.
Remember the promise you and I made
Down in the meadow, where we two met."

Well, Jessie chopped off the frog's head. And no sooner had she done so than up started the most handsome prince in the world. The prince married Jessie and the two of them were happy for as long as they lived.

CHARGER

"I'll just have to sell old Charger," said the farmer.

"Not Charger!" exclaimed his wife.

"He's one too many," the farmer said. "The other two are yearlings now."

So the farmer set off for the autumn Horse Fair. He rode Charger up the rainswept dale, feeling rather glum at the prospect of losing his loyal horse, and none too pleased at the thought of having to walk ten miles to get home again from the Fair.

In the high hills, the farmer met a pedlar, a small little man with a wrinkled face, dressed from top to toe in chestnut brown. He was struggling through the wind and rain, carrying a battered old suitcase.

"Would you sell your horse?" said the little man.

"That's just what I'm going to do," the farmer replied.

"How much?" asked the little man.

The farmer narrowed his eyes. "You could have him for

eight pounds," he said.

"No!" said the little man. "Not eight! I'll give you seven." And he dropped a hand into his pocket.

Well now, thought the farmer, *which is better: seven pounds for Charger here and now, or eight at the Fair — or seven, or six?* The farmer looked at the poor wet little man. He thought of the long walk home. "It's a deal," he said.

So the farmer dismounted and the man counted the coins into his hand: "One, two, three, four, five, six, seven."

"That's it," said the farmer.

Then the little man picked up his battered suitcase. He raised one foot as high as his hip, wedged it into a stirrup and swung up into the saddle.

And there and then, right in front of the round-eyed farmer, the little man and Charger sank into the earth.

THE DAUNTLESS GIRL

"Dang it!" said the farmer. "Not a drop left."

"Not one?" asked the blacksmith, raising his glass and inspecting it. His last inch of whisky glowed like molten honey in the flickering firelight.

"Why not?" said the miller.

"You fool!" said the farmer. "Because the bottle's empty." He peered into the flames. "Never mind that though," he said. "We'll send out my Mary. She'll go down to the inn and bring us another bottle."

"What?" said the blacksmith. "She'll be afraid to go out on such a dark night, all the way down to the village, and all on her own."

"Never!" said the farmer. "She's afraid of nothing—nothing live or dead. She's worth all my lads put together."

The farmer gave a shout and Mary came out of the kitchen. She stood and she listened. She went out into the dark night and in a little time returned with another bottle of whisky.

The miller and the blacksmith were delighted. They drank to her health, but later the miller said, "That's a strange thing, though."

"What's that?" asked the farmer.

"That she should be so bold, your Mary."

"Bold as brass," said the blacksmith. "Out and alone and the night so dark."

"That's nothing at all," said the farmer. "She'd go anywhere, day or night. She's afraid of nothing — nothing live or dead."

"Words," said the blacksmith. "But my, this whisky tastes good."

"Words nothing," said the farmer. "I bet you a golden guinea that neither of you can name anything that girl will not do."

The miller scratched his head and the blacksmith peered at the golden guinea of whisky in his glass. "All right," said the blacksmith. "Let's meet here again at the same time next week. Then I'll name something Mary will not do."

Next week the blacksmith went to see the priest and borrowed the key of the church door from him. Then he paid a visit to the sexton and showed him the key.

"What do you want with that?" asked the sexton.

"What I want with you," said the blacksmith, "is this. I want you to go into the church tonight, just before midnight, and hide yourself in the dead house."

"Never," said the sexton.

"Not for half a guinea?" asked the blacksmith.

The old sexton's eyes popped out of his head. "Dang it!" he said. "What's that for then?"

"To frighten that brazen farm girl, Mary," said the blacksmith, grinning. "When she comes to the dead house, just give a moan or a holler."

The old sexton's desire for the half guinea was even greater than his fear. He hummed and hawed and at last agreed to do as the blacksmith asked.

Then the blacksmith clumped the sexton on the back with his massive fist and the old sexton coughed. "I'll see you tomorrow," said the blacksmith, "and settle the account. Just before midnight, then! Not a minute later!"

The sexton nodded and the blacksmith strode up to the farm. Darkness was falling and the farmer and the miller were already drinking and waiting for him.

"Well?" said the farmer.

The blacksmith grasped his glass, then raised it and rolled the whisky around his mouth.

"Well," said the farmer. "Are you or aren't you?"

"This," said the blacksmith, "is what your Mary will not do. She won't go into the church alone at midnight . . ."

"No," said the miller.

". . . and go to the dead house," continued the blacksmith, "and bring back a skull bone. That's what she won't do."

"Never," said the miller.

The farmer gave a shout and Mary came out of the kitchen. She stood and she listened; and later, at midnight, she went out into the darkness and walked down to the church.

Mary opened the church door. She held up her lamp and clattered down the steps to the dead house. She pushed open its creaking door and saw skulls and thigh bones and bones of every kind gleaming in front of her. She stooped and picked up the nearest skull bone.

"Let that be," moaned a muffled voice from behind the dead house door. "That's my mother's skull bone."

So Mary put that skull down and picked up another.

"Let that be," moaned a muffled voice from behind the dead house door. "That's my father's skull bone."

So Mary put that skull bone down too and picked up yet another one. And, as she did so, she angrily called out, "Father or mother, sister or brother, I *must* have a skull bone and that's my last word." Then she walked out of the dead house, slammed the door, and hurried up the steps and back up to the farm.

Mary put the skull bone on the table in front of the farmer. "There's your skull bone, master," she said, and started off for the kitchen.

"Wait a minute!" said the farmer, grinning and shivering at one and the same time. "Didn't you hear anything in the dead house, Mary?"

"Yes," she said. "Some fool of a ghost called out to me: 'Let that be! That's my mother's skull bone' and 'Let that be! That's my father's skull bone.' But I told him straight: 'Father or mother, sister or brother, I *must* have a skull bone.'"

The miller and the blacksmith stared at Mary and shook their heads.

"So I took one," said Mary, "and here I am and here it is." She looked down at the three faces flickering in the firelight. "As I was going away," she said, "after I had locked the door, I heard the old ghost hollering and shrieking like mad."

The blacksmith and the miller looked at each other and got to their feet.

"That'll do then, Mary," said the farmer.

The blacksmith knew that the sexton must have been

scared out of his wits at being locked all alone in the dead house. They all raced down to the church, and clattered down the steps into the dead house, but they were too late. They found the old sexton lying stone dead on his face.

"That's what comes of trying to frighten a poor young girl," said the farmer. So the blacksmith gave the farmer a golden guinea and the farmer gave it to his Mary.

Mary and her daring were known in every house. And after her visit to the dead house, and the death of the old sexton, her fame spread for miles and miles around.

One day the squire, who lived three villages off, rode up to the farm and asked the farmer if he could talk to Mary.

"I've heard," said the squire, "that you're afraid of nothing."

Mary nodded.

"Nothing live or dead," said the farmer proudly.

"Listen then!" said the squire. "Last year my old mother died and was buried. But she will not rest. She keeps coming back into the house, and especially at mealtimes. Sometimes you can see her, sometimes you can't. And when you can't, you can still see a knife and fork get up off the table and play about where her hands would be."

"That's a strange thing altogether," said the farmer, "that she should go on walking."

"Strange and unnatural," said the squire. "And now my servants won't stay with me, not one of them. They're all afraid of her."

The farmer sighed and shook his head. "Hard to come by, good servants," he said.

"So," said the squire, "seeing as she's afraid of nothing, nothing live or dead, I'd like to ask your girl to come and work with me."

Mary was pleased at the prospect of such good employment and, sorry as he was to lose her, the farmer saw there was nothing for it but to let her go.

"I'll come," said the girl. "I'm not afraid of ghosts. But you ought to take account of that in my wages."

"I will," said the squire.

So Mary went back with the squire to be his servant. The first thing she always did was to lay a place for the ghost at table, and she took great care not to let the knife and fork lie criss-cross.

At meals, Mary passed the ghost the meat and vegetables and sauce and gravy. And then she said: "Pepper, madam?" and "Salt, madam?" The ghost of the squire's mother was pleased enough. Things went on the same from day to day until the squire had to go up to London to settle some legal business.

Next morning Mary was down on her knees, cleaning the parlour grate, when she noticed something thin and glimmering push in through the parlour door, which was just ajar; when it got inside the room, the shape began to swell and open out. It was the old ghost.

For the first time, the ghost spoke to the girl. "Mary," she said in a hollow voice, "are you afraid of me?"

"No, madam," said Mary. "I've no cause to be afraid of you, for you are dead and I'm alive."

For a while the ghost looked at the girl kneeling by the parlour grate. "Mary," she said, "will you come down into the cellar with me? You mustn't bring a light—but I'll shine enough to light the way for you."

So the two of them went down the cellar steps and the ghost shone like an old lantern. When they got to the bottom, they went down a passage, and took a right turn and a left, and then the ghost pointed to some loose tiles in one corner. "Pick up those tiles," she said.

Mary did as she was asked. And underneath the tiles were two bags of gold, a big one and a little one.

The ghost quivered. "Mary," she said, "that big bag is for your master. But that little bag is for you, for you are a dauntless girl and deserve it."

Before Mary could open the bag or even open her mouth, the old ghost drifted up the steps and out of sight. She was never seen again and Mary had a devil of a time groping her way along the dark passage and up out of the cellar.

After three days, the squire came back from London.

"Good morning, Mary," he said. "Have you seen anything of my mother while I've been away?"

"Yes, sir," said Mary. "That I have." She opened her eyes wide. "And if you aren't afraid of coming down into the cellar with me, I'll show you something."

The squire laughed. "I'm not afraid if you're not afraid," he said, for the dauntless girl was a very pretty girl.

So Mary lit a candle and led the squire down into the cellar, walked along the passage, took a right turn and a left, and raised the loose tiles in the corner for a second time.

"Two bags," said the squire.

"Two bags of gold," said Mary. "The little one is for you and the big one is for me."

"Lor!" said the squire, and he said nothing else. He did think that his mother might have given him the big bag, as indeed she had, but all the same he took what he could.

After that, Mary always crossed the knives and forks at mealtimes to prevent the old ghost from telling what she had done.

The squire thought things over: the gold and the ghost

and Mary's good looks. What with one thing and another he proposed to Mary, and the dauntless girl, she accepted him. In a little while they married, and so the squire did get both bags of gold after all.

THE PEDLAR OF SWAFFHAM

One night John Chapman had a dream.

A man stood by him, dressed in a surcoat as red as blood; and the man said, "Go to London Bridge. Go and be quick. Go, good will come of it."

John the pedlar woke with a start. "Cateryne," he whispered. "Cateryne, wake up! I've had a dream."

Cateryne, his wife, groaned and tossed and turned. "What?" she said.

"I've had a dream."

"Go to sleep, John," she said; and she fell asleep again.

John lay and wondered at his dream; and while he lay wondering he too fell asleep. But the man in scarlet came a second time, and said, "Go to London Bridge. Go and be quick. Go, good will come of it."

The pedlar sat up in the dark. "Cateryne!" he growled. "Wake up! Wake up! I've had the same dream again."

Cateryne tossed and turned. "What?" she said.

Then John told her his dream.

"You," she said, "you would believe anything."

The moment he woke next morning, the pedlar of Swaffham remembered his dream. He told it to his children, Margaret and Hue and Dominic. He told it to his wife again.

"Forget it!" said Cateryne.

So John went about his business as usual and, as usual, his mastiff went with him. He fed his pig and hens in the back yard. He hoisted his pack on his broad shoulders and went to the market-place; he set up his stall of pots and pans, household goods of one kind and another, phials and potions, special trimmings for ladies' gowns. He gossiped with his friends — the butcher, the baker, the smith, the shoemaker and the weaver, the dyer and many another. But no matter what he did, the pedlar could not escape his dream. He shook his lion-head, he rubbed his blue eyes, but the dream seemed real and everything else seemed dreamlike. "What am I to do?" he said.

And his mastiff opened his jaws, and yawned.

That evening John Chapman walked across the market-place to the tumbledown church. And there he found the thin priest, Master Fuller; his holy cheekbones shone in the half-light. "Well, what is it?" Master Fuller said.

Then John told him about his strange dream.

"I dream, you dream, everyone dreams," said the priest impatiently, swatting dust from his black gown. "Dream of how we can get gold to rebuild our church! This ramshackle place is an insult to God."

The two of them stood and stared sadly about them: all the walls of stone were rickety and uneven; the roof of the north aisle had fallen in, and through it they could see the crooked spire.

John Chapman gave a long sigh. "Gold," he said. "I wish I could."

Then the pedlar left the church and went back to his small cottage. But he was still uneasy. Nothing he did, and nothing anyone had said, seemed to make any difference; he could not forget his dream.

That night Cateryne said, "You've talked and talked of the man with the surcoat as red as blood. You've been more dreaming than awake. Perhaps, after all, you must go to London Bridge."

"I'll go," said John. "I'll go and be quick."

Next day, John Chapman got up at first light. At once he began to make ready for his journey. He hurried about, he banged his head against a beam, his face turned red. "I must take five gold pieces," he said. "I must take my cudgel."

"You must take your hood," said Cateryne.

Then John looked at his mastiff. "I must take you," he said. And the mastiff thumped the ground with his tail; dust and chaff flew through the air.

"Tell no one where I've gone," said John Chapman. "I don't want to be the laughing-stock of Swaffham."

Then, while the pedlar ate his fill of meat and curds, Cateryne put more food into his pack — cheese, and two loaves made of beans and bran, and a gourd full of ale.

So everything was ready. And just as the June sun rose behind a light cloud, a great coin of gold, John kissed his wife and his children goodbye.

"Come back," called little Dominic.

They stood by the door, the four of them, waving and waving until the pedlar with his pack, his cudgel and his mastiff, had walked out of Swaffham; out of sight.

John Chapman strode past the archery butts just outside

the town; he hurried between fields white with sheep. At first he knew the way well, but then the rough highway that men called the Gold Road left the open fields behind and passed through sandy heathland where there were no people, no sheep, no villages.

Soon the rain came, heavy, blurring everything. John pulled his hood over his head, but the water seeped through it. It soaked through his clothes, dripped from his nose.

By midday, he was tired and steaming. So he stopped to eat food and give a bone to his mastiff. And while they ate, some lord's messenger, decked out in red and blue, galloped by and spattered them with mud.

"The devil take him!" the pedlar said.

During the afternoon, the rain eased and the pedlar and his dog were able to quicken their pace. They made good progress; one by one, the milestones dropped away.

But that evening it grew dark before the pedlar could find any shelter, even a peasant's shack or some deserted hovel. John had no choice but to sleep in the open, under an oak tree. "God help us," he said, "if there are wolves."

But there were no wolves, only strange night sounds: the tree groaning and creaking, wind in the moaning leaves and wind in the rustling grass, the barking of fox and vixen. When first light came, John could barely get to his feet for the ache in his cold bones and the cramp in his empty stomach.

And his mastiff hobbled about as if he were a hundred.

So for four days they walked on. Every hour contained its own surprise; John talked to a friendly priest who had been to Jerusalem; he walked with a couple of vagabonds who wanted him to go to a fair at Waltham; he shook off a rascally pardoner who tried to sell him a ticket to heaven;

he saw rabbits, and hares, and deer; he gazed down from hill-crests at tapestries of fields; he followed the way through dark forests where only silence lived. Never in his life had John seen so many strangers nor set eyes on so many strange things. He said to his mastiff, "We're foreigners in our own country."

Sometimes the pedlar's pack chafed at his shoulders; often he envied the many travellers with horses — pilgrims and merchants, scholars and monks; but not for one moment did he forget his purpose. For as long as it was light, John Chapman made haste, following the Gold Road south towards London. And each night, after the first, he stayed at a wayside inn or in a monastery.

On the morning of the fifth day, the pedlar and his dog came at last to the City of London. At the sight of the high walls, the pedlar's heart quickened, and so did his step.

And his mastiff leaped about, barking for excitement.

They hurried through the great gate; and there before them were crowds of people coming and going, to-ing and fro-ing; men shouting their wares; women jostling, talking; small children begging; and many, many others sitting in rags in the filthy street. And there were houses to left and right; and after that, more houses, more streets, and always more people. John had never seen such a sight nor smelt such a stink nor heard such a hubbub.

A tide of people swept him along until he came to a place where four ways met. There, John stopped a man and asked him the way to London Bridge.

"Straight on," said the man. "Straight as an arrow's flight, all the way."

The broad river gleamed under the sun, silver and green, ruckled by wind; gulls swooped and climbed again, shrieking. The great bridge spanned the water, the long bridge with its houses overhanging the river. It was a sight to gladden any man. And when he saw it, John Chapman got to his knees. He thanked God that his journey had been safe, and that he had come at last to London Bridge.

But the moment the pedlar stepped on to the bridge itself he felt strangely foolish. All his hope and excitement seemed long ago. People were passing this way and that, but no one looked at John. No one took the least notice of him. Having at last found London Bridge, the poor pedlar of Swaffham felt utterly lost.

He walked up and down, he stared about him; he watched boats shoot the bridge; he added up his money. Hour after hour after hour went by; the pedlar waited.

Late that afternoon, a group of pilgrims, all with horses, gathered on the bridge. And they began to sing: *As you came from the holy-land of Walsingham . . .*

"Walsingham!" cried John. "I know it well. I've taken my wares there a hundred times. What does this song mean? Will *this* explain my dream?"

As if to answer him, the group of pilgrims broke up and rode off, still singing, even as he hurried towards them.

"Wait!" bawled John. "Wait!"

But the hooves of the horses clattered and the poor pedlar was left, in the fading light, looking after them.

John felt heavy-hearted. He knew there was nothing he could do until the next morning. He wearily asked of a passer-by where he might stay, and was directed to The Three Cranes, a hostelry on the riverside, a stopping-place for passengers coming down the river, a sleeping-place for travellers in all weathers.

There John Chapman and his mastiff shared a bed of straw; they were both dog-tired.

Early on the morning of the second day the pedlar and his dog returned to the bridge. Once again, hour after hour after hour went by. John felt foolish, then lonely, then hopeless, then angry.

Late that day he saw a man with matted red hair lead on to the bridge a loping black bear. "Look!" he exclaimed delightedly.

And his mastiff looked, carefully.

"A rare sight!" said John. "A sight worth travelling miles to see. Perhaps *this* is what I have travelled for. Perhaps here I shall find the meaning of my dream." And the pedlar greeted the man; he thought he had never seen anyone so ugly in all his life. "Does the bear dance?" he asked.

"He does," said the man. He squinted at John. "Give me gold and I'll show you."

"Another time," said the pedlar. He stooped to pat the bear's gleaming fur.

"Leave him alone!" snapped the man.

"Why?" asked John.

"He'll have your hand off, that's why."

The pedlar stepped back hastily and called his mastiff to heel.

"He had a hand off at Cambridge," said the man. "So you watch it! Hands off!"

"Not the best of travelling companions," said John.

"Mind your words," growled the man, and he squinted more fiercely than ever. "He'll bite your head off."

"Like you," said John. And with that, he walked away.

So the second day turned out no better than the first. And on the third day the poor pedlar waited and waited, he walked up and down and he walked to and fro, and no good came of it. "Now we have only one piece of gold left," he said to his mastiff. "Tomorrow we'll have to go home; I'm a great fool to have come at all."

At that moment a man shaped like an egg waddled up to John, and greeted him. "For three days," he said, "you've loitered on this bridge."

"How do you know?" asked John, surprised.

"I keep a shop here and I've seen you come and go, come and go from dawn to dusk." He narrowed his eyes. "What are you up to? Who are you waiting for?"

"That's exactly what I was asking myself," said the pedlar sadly. "To tell you the truth, I've walked to London Bridge because I dreamed that good would come of it."

"Lord preserve me!" exclaimed the shopkeeper. "What a waste of time!"

John Chapman shrugged his shoulders and sighed; he didn't know what to say.

"Only fools follow dreams," said the shopkeeper. "Why, last night I had a dream myself. I dreamed that a pot of gold lay buried by a hawthorn tree in a garden; and the garden belonged to some pedlar, in a place called Swaffham."

"A pot of gold?" said John. "A pedlar?"

"You see?" said the egg-shaped man. "Nonsense!"

"Yes," said John.

"Dreams are just dreams," said the shopkeeper with a wave of his pudgy hand. "You're wasting your time. Take my advice and go back home."

"I will!" said John Chapman.

So it was that, in the evening of the twelfth day after his departure, John Chapman and his dog—spattered with mud, aching and blistered, weary but excited—returned home. They saw the leaning church spire; they passed the archery butts; they came at last to John's small cottage of wattle and daub.

Cateryne had never in her life been so glad to see her husband.

Margaret and Hue leaped about and their ashen hair danced on their heads. "Come back!" cried little Dominic.

"So," asked Cateryne, "what of the dream, John?"

Then John told them in his own unhurried way. He told them of his journey; he told them of the long days on London Bridge; and, at last, he told them of the shop-keeper's words.

"A man follows a dream and returns with another man's dream," said Cateryne. "That's very strange. And how can it be true?"

"I've asked myself that a thousand times," the pedlar said, "and there's only one way to find out."

The gnarled hawthorn tree stood at the end of the yard; it had lived long, perhaps hundreds of years. And now its leaves seemed to whisper secrets.

Then hens clucked in the dusk; and the pig lay still, one eye open, watching John.

"I'll start here," said the pedlar quietly. Then he gripped his round-edged spade and began to dig, firmly, rhythmically, making a mound of the loose earth.

"Can I?" asked Margaret.

"Let me!" said Hue.

"No!" said John. "Wait!" And again he dug, firmly, rhythmically. The spade bit into the packed soil.

At once they heard it, they all heard it together, the grind of metal against metal, muted by soil. The pedlar took one look at his family and began to dig as fast as he could. Earth flew through the air. "Look!" gasped the pedlar. "Look! Look!" He had partly uncovered a great metal pot.

John tossed away his spade. He bent down and tugged. He worked his fingers further under the pot and tugged again. Then suddenly the dark earth gave up its secret. John staggered backwards, grasping the pot, and, as he fell, the lid flew off. Coins rained on the pedlar's face; the ground was carpeted with gold.

They were all utterly silent, dumbfounded. Only the tree, the tree in the gloom went on whispering.

"John, John, what shall we do with it?" said Cateryne.

"Gather it up," said the pedlar, slapping earth and straw from his surcoat with his great hands. "Take it inside."

They picked up the gold coins and put them back into the pot, and together carried it into their cottage. There they placed it on the floor, in front of the fire.

"Look! What's this?" said Hue, lifting the lid off the pot, and rubbing it. "It's writing."

John took the lid from him and frowned over it. "Yes," he said slowly, shaking his head. "It's words." Then John smiled. "I know," he said. "I'll hide the gold here and take the empty pot with the rest of my wares to the market-place. Someone is sure to come along and read it for us."

Next morning the pedlar was early in the market-place, standing over his wares with his elder children and his dog. In no time Master Fuller came picking his way towards them through the higgledy-piggledy stalls — a dark figure amongst bright colours, a silent man in a sea of noise. "John Chapman," he exclaimed. "Where have you been?"

"To and fro," said the pedlar. "To and fro."

"And where were you last Sunday?" asked the priest. "I missed you at Mass."

"Well, I . . ."

"Excuses! Always excuses!" said the priest sharply. "Who shall be saved? Men are empty vessels." And he rapped the great metal pot with his knuckles; it rang with a fine deep note. "Now that's a fine vessel!" said Master Fuller.

"It is," agreed John Chapman.

"There are words on it," said the priest. He raised the lid and narrowed his eyes.

The pedlar looked at him anxiously.

"It's in Latin," said Master Fuller. "It says, *Under me . . .* yes . . . *Under me there lies another richer than I.*" The priest frowned. "What does that mean?" he said.

John Chapman scratched the back of his head.

"Where did you get it?"

"Out of a back yard," said the pedlar, shrugging his broad shoulders.

"I must go," said the priest suddenly. "All this idle chatter. Men would do better to give time to God." And with that, the priest walked off towards the rickety church.

At once, the pedlar packed up his wares and, led by his children, followed by his mastiff, he hurried home.

"This time you shall dig," the pedlar told his children.

Then Hue grasped the spade and began to dig; the rounded edge sheared through the darkness. His face soon flushed; he began to pant.

"Now let Margaret have it," the pedlar said.

Hue scowled, and handed the spade to his sister.

Then Margaret threw back her hair and stepped into the pit, and dug yet deeper. Deeper and deeper. Then, once again, metal grated against metal—the same unmistakable sound. Margaret shivered with excitement. "You," she said, and handed the spade back to her father.

Once more John dug as fast as he could; once more he

tugged and tugged; and once more the reluctant earth yielded its secret — a second great pot, an enormous pot twice as large as the first. The pedlar could barely heave it out of the hole and on to the level ground. When he levered off the lid, they all saw that this pot too was heaped to the brim with glowing gold. "It's like a dream," said John, "and because of a dream. But we're awake, and rich."

Cateryne stared into the gaping black hole. "Who could have hidden it there?" she said. "And why?"

"How shall we ever know?" replied the pedlar. "Someone who once lived here? Travellers on the Gold Road? How can we tell? People always say the hawthorn tree is a magic tree."

"And what are we going to do with it?" asked Cateryne.

For a moment John did not reply. His blue eyes closed, his face wrinkled. "I know," he said at last. "I know. A little we'll keep — enough to pay for our own small needs, enough to buy ourselves a strip of land. But all the rest, every coin, we must give to Master Fuller to build the new church."

Cateryne drew in her breath and smiled and clapped her hands. "Amen!" she said.

"Amen!" chimed the children.

"In this way," said John, "everyone in Swaffham will share in the treasure."

"Now," said Cateryne, "and in time to come."

That afternoon, John Chapman found the priest skulking in the gloom of the tumbledown church. "Master Fuller," he said, "I can give gold for the new church."

"Every piece counts," said the priest.

"I have many," said John.

"Many?" said the priest suspiciously.

"Wait here," said the pedlar. He hurried out of the

church and back to his cottage. There, he counted out one hundred pieces of gold for his own needs and the needs of his family, and hid them in the inner room, under the bed of straw.

Then the pedlar and his wife, and Margaret and Hue, followed by Dominic and their loyal mastiff, carried the hoard to Swaffham Church. As they crossed the market-place, they shouted to their friends, "Come with us! Come to the church!"

So the butcher, the baker, the smith, the shoemaker, and the weaver, the dyer and many another left their work. And in no time, a great procession, curious and chattering, were filing into the silent church.

In the nave, John and Cateryne turned their pot upside down. Margaret and Hue did the same. A great mound of coins glowed mysteriously in the half-light.

The townspeople gasped and Master Fuller's bony face cracked into a grin; his eyes gleamed. "Explain!" he said.

So John Chapman told them the whole story from beginning to end. And no storyteller, before or since, has ever had such an audience.

Then the priest rubbed his hands. "There's enough gold here," he said, "to rebuild the north aisle, and the steeple."

The townsfolk began to whisper excitedly.

Then the priest raised his hand, and he said, "Let us pray, and, after that . . . let us sing and dance the night away."

"Sing in the churchyard? Dance in the churchyard?" everyone cried.

"Even until this old church falls down," said Master Fuller. And for the first time that anyone could remember, he laughed. He threw back his head and laughed.

So, that same evening, a man with a bugle and a man with a humstrum and a man with cymbals and clappers played as if they meant to raise the roof off every house in Swaffham; the townsfolk sang and danced until midnight. And John the dreamer was tossed by the dancers into the air, higher and higher, towards the stars.

And his mastiff sat on his haunches, and laughed.

THE CHANGELING

Last week there was a wonder.

Up at Hawes's there was a birth, a son to follow four bonny daughters. Such a scowl of a night, but no one was paying any attention to that. There was singing and dancing, all the neighbours in.

They swaddled him in a mesh of muslin,
They swathed him in pure rainbow silk . . .

That was the Tuesday, and they arranged with me to baptise the bairn on the Sabbath.

But Saturday morning there was a horrible yelling coming out of the cradle. And when Mrs. Hawes looked in, she saw her bairn had turned yellow and ugly. His nose was a sort of snout, his milkskin had become leathery, and his teeth were already coming through.

Mrs. Hawes cried out, and the farmer and his neighbours, they all rubbed their eyes. It made no difference, of course. The little bairn just lay there and squinted up at them and threshed its legs, and yelled.

Poor Mrs. Hawes, she's a fragile woman and she was in a terrible state. When she tried to feed the bairn, he tore at her poor breasts. He wrestled around, and groused and grizzled and, one way and another, the farmer and his family were unable to get a minute's sleep for the next three nights.

That was when they sent for my lass Janey, and asked her to try her hand. She knows what's what, Janey, just like her mother. She won't stand any nonsense.

Out trooped the farmer and his family, and off to the market. They were all heartily glad to see the back of the little bairn, and to get the sound of that yammering out of their ears.

Janey promised Mrs. Hawes she would be patient. After all . . . the poor wee bairn, it was so ugly and so sad, and seemed so unhappy with this bright world.

But what with all the weeping and wailing, Janey finally lost her temper. She yelled right back at the bairn, and told him that his mewling was stopping her from winnowing the corn and grinding the meal.

The bairn looked up then and opened its eyes as wide as can be. "Well, Janey," it said, clear as clear, with a knowing look. "Well, Janey, loose the cradle-band! Watch out for your neighbours and I'll work your work."

Then that wee devil climbed out of his cradle. He stretched and grinned and strolled out of the house. He cut the corn, he fed the livestock in the fields; then the wind got up and the mill began to turn . . .

Janey's knees were knocking together. She wasn't going to show it, though. She knew that would only turn bad into worse. So when the wee devil had finished the work and strolled back into the house again, she fed him and played with him until the farmer and his family came home.

As soon as she saw them out of the window, Janey popped the bairn back into the cradle. And at that, the caterwauling began all over again.

Then Janey took Mrs. Hawes down to the kitchen and told her straight out what had happened. Poor Mrs. Hawes! "What shall I do, Janey? Help me, Janey!"

"The wee devil!" said Janey. "Leave him to me! I'll cook some trouble for him."

At midnight, Janey asked Hawes if he would climb up on to the farmhouse roof and lay three bricks across part of the top of the chimney pot, and she told his wife to work the bellows until the fire was glowing — a bed of red hot coals.

Then my lass, she stripped that wee scrap, she undressed him and threw him on to the burning coals.

The little wee fellow shrieked and he screamed.

At once there was a rustling sound, quickly growing, like wind before rain. And then a rattling at the windows and tapping, tapping at the chimney and banging at the farmhouse doors. That was the fairies, right enough.

"In the name of God," shouted Janey, "bring back the bairn!"

Darkness and wind! The casement window screeched. They brought back the bairn then; they laid him safely in his mother's lap.

And the wee devil? He flew up the chimney laughing.

THE WISE MEN OF GOTHAM

1 Two men from Gotham met on Nottingham Bridge. One of them was on his way to the market to buy sheep and the other was on his way home.

"Good morning!" said the man coming from the village.

"Where are you going?" said the man coming from the market.

"Market!" said the first man. "I'm going to buy some sheep."

"Sheep!" said the other. "How will you get them home?"

"Over this bridge, of course," said the first man.

"By Robin Hood," said the second man, "you will not!"

"By Maid Marian," said the first, "I certainly will!"

"You will not," said the second man.

"I will," said the first.

Then the two men began to hammer the ground with their staves. They pounded the cobbles and the bridge boomed.

"Keep your sheep back!" the first man shouted.

"Beware!" yelled the second. "Beware or mine will leap over the parapet!"

"My sheep will all come home this way," bawled the first man.

"They will not!" shouted the other.

While they were arguing, another wise man from Gotham rode up to the bridge on his way home from the market. He had a sack of meal up in the saddle behind him.

For a while this man listened to his neighbours arguing about their sheep, with not one sheep in sight. Then he jumped down from his horse. "You fools!" he called. "Will you never learn sense?"

The man's two neighbours turned and looked at him.

"Come on!" he said. "Help me get this sack up on to my shoulder."

When the man with the meal had shouldered his sack, he went over to the parapet, untied the sack's mouth, and shook out all the meal into the river. "How much meal is there in this sack?" he asked.

"None," said the first man.

"None," said the second man.

"There's just as much meal in this sack," said the wise man, "as you have wit in your two heads, arguing over sheep you don't even own."

So which of these three men was the wisest?

2 "That cuckoo," said the boys of Gotham. "Let's capture it and then we'll be able to hear it sing all year round."

So the boys made a circular hedge and then they caught the cuckoo and put her into it.

"Here you are," said one.

"And here you'll stay," said another, "and sing all the year round."

"Otherwise," said a third, "you'll have nothing to eat or drink."

The cuckoo looked at the boys. She looked at the circuit of the hedge, and spread her wings and flew away.

"Curses!" shouted the boys. "We'll get her! We didn't make our hedge high enough."

3 Twelve men from Gotham made up a fishing party. Some of them fished from the bank of the stream; a few of them waded into the water—right up to their shins.

Before they left for home, one of the men said, "What an adventure we've had today, wading and all! I hope to God none of us have been drowned."

"Let's check before we leave," said another man. "There were twelve of us set out from home."

So each man counted his neighbours and every one of them counted up to eleven.

"One of us is missing," they said. "One of us has been drowned."

The men walked up and down the little stream where they had been fishing, looking for the missing man, wringing their hands, and sighing and moaning.

At this moment, one of the king's courtiers rode up.

"What's wrong?" he asked. "What are you looking for?"

"Oh!" cried the men. "We've been fishing here today. Twelve of us! One of us has been drowned."

"You count," said the courtier. "One of you count again and I'll check."

So one man walked round and counted his neighbours.

But he did not count himself.

"Well!" said the courtier. "Well! Well! What will you give me if I can find the twelfth man?"

"All the money in my pocket!" said one man.

"All mine too!" cried another.

The wise men of Gotham promised to give the courtier every coin they had on them.

"All right!" said the courtier. "Give me the money!"

As the courtier walked round the group, collecting the money, he thwacked each man over the shoulders with his whip and began to count, "One, two, three . . ." When the courtier came to the last man, he thwacked him especially hard and called out, "Here he is! Here's the twelfth man!"

The wise men rubbed their shoulders. "God bless you!" they said. "You've found our friend and neighbour."

4 A man from Gotham was on his way to the market at Nottingham to sell his cheeses. On his way down the hill to Nottingham Bridge, one of the cheeses toppled out of his shoulder bag and ran down the hill.

"Ah!" said the man. "So you're able to run down the hill on your own." He looked at the cheese, rolling and cartwheeling down the slope, and it started him thinking. "In that case," he said, "I expect the other cheeses can run too. I'll get them all to run down the hill."

So the wise man swung the heavy bag off his shoulders, and took out the cheeses, and sent them tumbling down the hill one after another. One disappeared into a thorn bush, one rolled into a rabbit-hole, one ran into a thicket. The man wagged a finger at the disappearing cheeses. "Make sure," he shouted, "that you all meet me in the market-place!"

The man stayed at Nottingham market until it was almost over. Then he made his way round, asking friends and strangers alike whether they had seen his cheeses.

"Why?" asked another man from Gotham. "Who is bringing them?"

"They are!" said the man. "They're bringing themselves."

"Bringing themselves!"

"And they know the way well enough, damn them!" exclaimed the man. "When I saw my cheeses running so fast, I was afraid that they would overrun this market-place. I should think they're almost in York by now."

So the man spent what money he had with him on the loan of a horse. He rode after his cheeses. He galloped all the way to York.

But no one has been able to find out where the cheeses got to, not from that day to this.

5 A woman of Gotham was walking home from a neighbour's cottage late at night. In fact, it was after midnight.

As she passed the horse-pond, she saw a whole green cheese floating just under the surface.

"My word!" she exclaimed. "This is worth some effort."

She ran back to her cottage, shouting as she went. Her husband heard her and all her neighbours, lying in their beds, heard her too. They jumped up, they opened their little windows.

"There's a green cheese in the pond," bawled the woman. "Come and help me rake it out!"

The woman's friends and neighbours hurried out of their little cottages in their nightshirts and nightcaps. They all brought their rakes and began to drag the surface of the pond.

Just then a passing cloud sank the cheese. The woman sighed a deep sigh and all her neighbours went back to their beds, disappointed.

KING OF THE CATS

I suppose I can think myself lucky. There's plenty in our village who are drawing unemployment, and I know two more—three if you count Dan, he's taking early retirement—who reckon they'll be laid off before Christmas. At least people need me; and they always will.

It's not all laughs, mind. The only ones who thank you are the early birds. And then you're all on your own, and you're out in every weather, too. And the old flowers, the pulpy heaps of them, they smell sickly sweet!

You get some weird experiences, I can tell you. Weird and wonderful!

One evening last summer I was out late; the vicar said they needed it for nine in the morning. I was having my break, sitting on the edge like, and swinging my legs. Well, I took a nip or two and I was so tired that I reckon I fell asleep.

A cat woke me up. "Miaou!" And when I opened my old eyes, it was almost dark and I was down at the bottom.

I stood up and peered over the edge and you know what I saw? Nine black cats! They all had white chests and they were coming down the path, carrying a coffin covered with black velvet. My! Oh my! I kept very quiet but I still had a careful look. There was a little gold crown sitting on top of the black velvet. And at every third step the cats all paused, solemn like, and cried "Miaou!"

Then the cats turned off the path and headed straight towards me. Their eyes were shining, luminous and green. Eight of them were carrying the coffin and a big one walked in front of them, showing them the way. One step, two steps, three steps: miaou!

When they got to the graveside, they stopped. They all looked straight at me. My! Oh my! I felt queer.

Then the big cat, the one at the front, stepped towards me. "Tell Dildrum," he said in a squeaky voice, "tell Dildrum," he said, "that Doldrum is dead."

Then he turned his back on me and led away the other cats with the coffin. One step, two steps, three steps: miaou!

As soon as they were out of the way, I scrambled out of the grave, and I was glad to get home, I can tell you. There they all were: my Mary cross-eyed with knitting and Mustard hopping around his cage and old Sam stretched out in the corner. Everything as usual; the clock ticking on the mantelpiece.

So I told the old girl about the talking cat and the coffin and the crown. She gave me one of those looks — a sort of gleam behind her specs.

"Yes, Harry," she said.

"It's true, Mary," I said. "I couldn't have made it up. And who is Dildrum anyhow?"

"How should I know?" said Mary. "That's enough of your stories. You're upsetting old Sam."

Old Sam got up. First he prowled around and then he looked straight at me. My! Oh my! I felt very queer again.

"That's just what the cat said," I said. "Not a word more and not a word less. He said, 'Tell Dildrum that Doldrum is dead.' But how can I? How can I tell Dildrum that Doldrum is dead if I don't know who Dildrum is?"

"Stop, Harry!" shouted Mary. "Look at old Sam! Look!"

Old Sam was sort of swelling. Swelling and staring right through me. And at last he shrieked out, "Doldrum — old Doldrum dead? Then I'm the King of the Cats!"

He leaped into the fireplace and up the chimney, and he has never been seen again.

THE DARK HORSEMAN

As Jemmy strode down the road towards Slane, he began to say praises.

"Praise be and I'm Irish," he said, and he swiped at a clump of nettles with his shillelagh. "Praise be and it's the top of the summer."

Jemmy's trousers flapped at his step, and by the wayside poppies and cornflowers nodded and smouldered and beckoned.

"My cattle are sleek," said Jemmy. "They're buttery creatures! They'll sell well at the fair. And then I'll drink a whiskey, and take a turn on the whirly horses, and talk to a girl with stars in her eyes."

Jemmy Nowlan managed an estate outside Slane, and he had sent ahead his cattle early that morning. Jemmy was tall; he was very strong; he was handsome and he knew it.

"Praise be and I'm alive," he said. "Praise be and praise be and I'm Jemmy Nowlan."

While Jemmy was crossing the lonely heath just outside

Slane, the clouds began to gather over his head. The summer's day that had begun with scents and sunlight and soft dawdling wind turned beetle-browed and bellowing.

Then Jemmy heard the clop-clop of a horse coming up behind him. He turned round and saw a young dash of a man riding on a black horse: black velvet jacket, white ruffles at his wrists, starched wing collar, shiny black boots. Jemmy looked up and saw the man was swarthy, his skin was almost dark.

"Jemmy Nowlan," said the dark horseman. "I've been looking for you all along the road."

Jemmy Nowlan looked startled. He was sure he had never seen the man before.

"Come on up!" said the man. "There's a storm in the sky. I'll take you to the fair at Slane."

Jemmy didn't want to ride with the man. Not at all. He began to feel quite nervous of him, and gripped his shillelagh.

"Ach!" he said, looking up at the black sky and wrinkling his nose. "The weather'll be all right again soon."

And as he spoke, Jemmy could hear distant voices inside his head. He had to close his eyes to make out what they were saying: "Still such a young man and just whisked away . . . they took him into the heart of the hill . . . a prisoner, a prisoner . . . and the only times they ever saw him was along with the walking dead . . ."

"I'm going there myself." The voice of the horseman brought Jemmy back from his reverie. "And I'd be glad of your company, Jemmy Nowlan."

"Ach!" said Jemmy. "It's not for the likes of me to ride with the likes of you."

"I insist!" said the dark horseman.

Then he stooped and just touched one of Jemmy's

shoulders with his ivory whip. And the next thing Jemmy knew, he was mounted behind the dark horseman, and the horse was galloping like a storm of wind.

The horseman said nothing. He rode until the horse was sweating and foaming. He rode across wild heathland where Jemmy had never been before, and on into an oak forest, and up to a castle set in a green glade.

As they cantered over the drawbridge, Jemmy saw that dozens of servants were standing on the steps around the massive door, waiting to welcome them. They all wore the same livery—green and gold—and all of them were even smaller than the two dwarfs at Slane fair.

"Well!" they cried. "If it's not Jemmy Nowlan! Welcome, Jemmy Nowlan!" Scrambling around him and standing on each other's shoulders like a troupe of acrobats, they helped Jemmy dismount; they dusted him down; they put a drink in his fist; they asked what they could do for him.

"Very civil!" said Jemmy, and he took off his jaunting hat and ran a hand through his thick black hair. "Very civil!"

Then Jemmy saw a man waiting on the steps. He stood at least as high as Jemmy's hip and he was wearing a sumptuous outfit of purple and gold. *So, Jemmy Nowlan,* Jemmy thought, *the lord himself has come out to greet you.*

"Take Jemmy to his room," said the lord. "Let him dress."

Several servants escorted Jemmy to his room high in the castle, where his new clothes were waiting for him: a fine suit of brown velvet, and a cap and feather. Jemmy looked at them in admiration and delight.

Far from leaving him to look after himself, the green-and-gold servants would not allow Jemmy to lift a finger.

They took off his jacket and his shirt and his trousers, untied his shoes, and washed him after his journey.

"Blessings!" exclaimed Jemmy. "There's nothing wrong with this."

When the little servants had dressed Jemmy in his resplendent new outfit, they hurried him down a flight of circular stone steps and trotted beside him along dim passageways and led him into the castle hall.

This hall was hung with Chinese lanterns and garlands of flowers. Down at the far end, a group of musicians were playing fiddles and the little people were dancing.

"There's a sight!" said Jemmy. "I've never seen anything so lovely."

Most lovely of all were the ladies, with their flashing smiles, and their throats and fingers all covered in jewels. Jemmy couldn't take his eyes off them.

"Will you dance with me, Jemmy Nowlan?" asked one lady.

"No, Jemmy!" said another. "You must dance with me."

And like a hundred winter sparrows and a hunk of bread, all the ladies in the hall pecked and squabbled over which of them should dance with Jemmy Nowlan in his brown velvet suit.

"Blessings!" cried Jemmy. "I'll dance with you all."

And that is what he did. He danced with every single lady in the room, until he was so tired that the only thing he wanted to do was to lie down there and then, and go to sleep.

"You can take Jemmy Nowlan to his room," said the lord, "and put him to bed. But first he must tell me a story."

"Ach!" said Jemmy. "I don't know a story. I don't

know a story or I can't remember one. I was never any good at books."

"Shame on you, Jemmy!" said the lord.

"I'm very tired now, your lordship," said Jemmy. "Let me lie down and go to sleep."

"Sleep!" said the lord. "Not if I can help it." He signalled to a little red-headed man. "Throw Jemmy out!" he shouted. "He can't tell a story. I won't have anyone in this castle who can't tell me a story. Throw him out! He's not worth his supper."

So the red-headed man pushed Jemmy through the great castle door and down the steps and over the drawbridge to the edge of the oak forest.

Jemmy found a bench there and it was long enough for him to lie on. He had just stretched himself out and put his head in the pillow of one palm when three men stepped towards him through the dim lights of the wood. They were carrying a coffin.

Jemmy quickly sat up again.

"Oho!" said the men. "It's Jemmy Nowlan! He's just the man! We need a fourth man to carry this coffin."

So Jemmy fell into step with the three men and shouldered his share of the coffin. They walked through the forest. They brushed through hedges and stumbled over ditches, they tramped over firm fields and plunged through treacherous peat-bogs, until at last they reached an old churchyard at the head of a valley. It was overgrown with long grasses, and the graves were green with moss and lichen. Here the procession stopped. The three men and Jemmy laid down the coffin.

"Who'll dig the grave?" asked one man.

"We must draw lots," replied their leader.

Jemmy Nowlan drew the short straw. The three men

found him an old rusty spade, and he dug and he dug all night until the grave was gaping — six foot long and two foot wide and eight foot deep.

When Jemmy had all but finished, the leader of the group walked up and stood at the edge of the grave.

"This won't do," he said. "Not at all. This is never the place for a grave."

"Why not?" said Jemmy.

"I'll have no one buried here," said the leader. "My own father's bones lie in this churchyard."

So the three men and Jemmy had to shoulder the coffin again. They tramped over firm fields and plunged through the treacherous peat-bogs until they reached a second churchyard.

"Jemmy Nowlan," said the leader, "you must begin again."

"Curses!" said Jemmy. But the three men stood round him so that their shadows fell on to his in the moonlight, and he knew that he had no choice in the matter.

When Jemmy had finished digging the grave, one of the men asked, "And who shall we put in the coffin?"

"No need to draw lots!" said the leader. "Lay Jemmy Nowlan in the coffin."

The three men grabbed Jemmy and tried to throw him to the ground.

Jemmy yelled, and wrestled; he landed huge punches on all three men. Had they been merely human, they would ever have been able to withstand them. But after a while Jemmy felt himself weakening, and still it was three-to-one.

Then Jemmy saw that the leader had a forked hazel twig tucked into his belt. He bared his teeth. He shook like a dog. He jerked one arm free and grabbed the twig.

"I have it!" shouted Jemmy. He leaped up and whirled the twig round his head three times and then struck each of his enemies with it.

That was the end of the fight. The three men fell backwards and rolled over and lay face down in the dew. None of them even twitched a finger.

The coffin stood apart, gleaming white in the moonlight. No hand touched it; and no voice spoke.

Jemmy ran out of the churchyard. He had one thought in his mind, and that was to put as much distance as he could between himself and the three men, in case they should rise up again. Still holding the hazel twig in his right hand, he ran straight over the firm fields and zigzagged over the peat-bogs, he worked his way through hedges of briar and thorn, until he found himself standing in front of the castle again.

As Jemmy crossed the drawbridge, dozens of green-and-gold servants came out to meet him, as they had done before.

"Welcome!" they cried. "Welcome, Jemmy Nowlan! Come on in now! His lordship is waiting for you."

The servants led Jemmy down dim passageways and into a room where the lord of the castle was reclining on a velvet couch. "Ah, Jemmy!" he said. "You've come back. You've come back with a story after all."

"Ach!" said Jemmy.

"I allow no one in this castle to eat or drink or sleep until they've told me something—something wonderful that's happened to them."

Jemmy began to smile. "In that case," he said, "in that case, my lord, I can tell you a wonderful story: the most wonderful of all."

"You can begin now," said the lord.

"There was a man," said Jemmy, "and he was very tired. He was as tired as a dog. So he stretched out on a bench. He pillowed his head in the palm of one hand. But before he had even closed his eyes, up stepped three men through the dim lights of the wood. They were carrying a coffin . . ."

The lord listened to every word and at the end of the tale he clapped his hands. "A long journey," he cried, "and a grim load! That's a very fine story. A story of death-in-life," said the lord, "and life-in-death. You've earned your supper." He clapped his hands for a second time and a succession of servants carried in food on golden dishes and crystal cups filled with wine.

"Eat and drink whatever you like," said the lord. "It is all for you."

Jemmy Nowlan was ravenous. With his right hand he still held the magic hazel twig and with his left he ate and drank. When he had finished, Jemmy felt very strange and then rather dazed. He got up from the table but at once he reeled sideways and he toppled over. He lay on the ground completely and utterly dead to the world.

"Where am I?" groaned Jemmy. "My head! Where am I at all?"

He was lying up against a haystack and half-a-dozen hens were prinking around him.

Jemmy screwed up his eyes against the morning sunlight. "Curses!" he said. "The sun's bright this morning." Then he looked at his crumpled clothing; the brown velvet suit, the cap and the feather, they were gone, all gone.

"Ach!" said Jemmy in disgust. "I'll get even with them. That dark horseman!"

Jemmy sat up on one elbow. "Nasty things!" he said.

"Bad and shabby, stopping me from selling my cattle, and they already at the fair. Ah!" sighed Jemmy. "They could have left me that brown velvet suit."

When he stood up, Jemmy saw that he had been asleep under one of his own hayricks, no more than a hundred yards from the comfort of his own bed.

"Devil take them!" said Jemmy. "Nasty and spiteful, that's what they are! Envious things!"

Then Jemmy saw the forked hazel twig; he was still holding it in his right hand. He looked at the shine-and-shimmer of the world around him. "Blessings!" he said. "Praise be and I'm alive," he said.

THE BLACK BULL OF NORWAY

At another time (and that time was long ago) and in another country (and the country was Norway), there was a poor mountain woman whose husband died while their three daughters were still small children.

The woman was determined her daughters should lack for nothing. She worked all day and half the night. The girls' dresses were simple and pretty; their food was nourishing; and the little cottage where they had always lived was as clean as a cat's tongue.

In the summer the girls brought back wildflowers from the meadows every day and slipped one through the handle of each mug and jug on the dresser, and tucked them through the collars of their three swishing cows, and arranged a bunch on the middle of the scoured table.

As the girls grew up, they saw their mother had paid a price for all her hard work: her green youth and gaiety. They felt sorry and indignant for her and, like fledglings, they began to grow restless.

"I'll go down to the valley," said the eldest daughter, whose name was Betony. "Who knows whom I'll meet? Who knows where I'll go?"

The woman baked her daughter a barley-cake and a good wedge of gammon. Then Betony walked over the mountain slopes, through a pine forest, and down to a cottage far below — the home of the wise woman and her only daughter.

"Stay here today," said the wise woman. "Go and look out of the back door and see what you can see."

"Nothing!" said Betony. "Nothing out of the way."

The eldest daughter saw nothing on the second day either. But on the third day she saw six horses drawing a glassy coach towards the cottage.

"There's a coach-and-six coming," called Betony.

"Ah!" said the wise woman. "That's coming for you."

So one of the coachmen dismounted and opened the glass door for the eldest daughter, and they galloped away.

It wasn't very long before the second daughter, whose name was Bracken, wanted to follow in her elder sister's footsteps.

"Mother!" she said. "Bake me a barley-cake and a wedge of gammon! I'll walk down to the valley. Who knows whom I'll meet? Who knows where I'll go?"

Bracken called at the wise woman's cottage, just as her sister had done. She looked out of the back door, and on the third day she saw four greys drawing a silver coach towards the cottage.

"There's a coach-and-four coming," called Bracken.

"Ah!" said the wise woman. "That's coming for you."

So the coachman dismounted and opened the glass door for the second daughter, and they galloped away.

"Mother!" said the youngest daughter, whose name was Flora. "Bake me a barley-cake and a wedge of gammon! I'll walk down to the valley."

"You too?" said her mother.

"Who knows whom I'll meet?" said Flora. "Who knows where I'll go?"

Flora took her leave of her mother and picked her way over the mountain and through the forest and down to the cottage of the wise woman.

"Go and look out of the back door," said the wise woman, "and see what you can see."

"Nothing," said Flora. "Nothing out of the way."

The youngest daughter saw nothing on the second day either. But on the third day she saw a huge black bull bucking and bellowing its way down towards the cottage.

"There's a black bull coming," called Flora, "and it's a big one."

"Ah!" said the wise woman. "That's coming for you."

"For me!" cried the girl. And her eyes brimmed with tears.

But the bull waited outside the cottage, and the wise woman helped the youngest daughter up on to its back, and away they went.

The black bull was an ugly great beast. His shoulders were broad, his eyes were bloodshot and his hair was matted and rough.

"Take hold of my horns, Flora," said the bull.

Flora leaned forward and gripped the bull's horns and at once the bull began to charge over the slopes. He jumped across a stream; he kicked up scree which went bumping and leaping down the mountainside behind them.

After a while, Flora's fear gave way to curiosity. The

black bull was travelling at a great pace and taking her into a remote and rocky area. For hour after hour he ran on without shortening his stride.

"I'm hungry," said Flora.

"There's food in my right ear," said the black bull.

"And thirsty," said Flora.

"And there's drink in my left ear. Eat and drink as much as you want."

So Flora ate and drank, and she felt wonderfully refreshed.

Quite late in the evening, as a chill damp mountain mist began to rise and fall around them, Flora saw a castle that seemed to grow straight out of rock. It was all parapets and pinnacles and peephole windows.

"That's where we'll stay tonight," the bull said. "My eldest brother lives there."

"Who are you, then?" said Flora.

But the bull did not reply; he galloped up to the castle courtyard.

Servants helped poor Flora down from the bull's back and escorted her into the castle, and then they ushered the bull into a pasture flanked by mountain-ash and sweet-smelling pine.

Flora ate well and slept well and in the morning a servant conducted her into a small and shining room that led out of the great hall. A man was sitting at the head of a long chestnut table.

"You've been welcome here," said the man, and Flora saw he was holding a most beautiful apple. It glowed as if lit by its own inner light.

"This apple is for you," said the man. "And you must not break it or open it until you have great need of it."

Then the castle servants lifted Flora on to the bull's

back. Away they went, and in the evening, after they had travelled many, many miles, they came to a castle alive with fluttering flags. There were flags surrounding it and flags on the keep and flags sticking out of almost every window.

"That's where we'll stay tonight," the bull said. "My elder brother lives there."

"Who are you, then?" said Flora.

But the bull did not reply; he galloped up to the castle courtyard.

Servants lifted Flora down from the bull's back, and ushered the bull into a pasture for the night. Then, in the morning, a servant conducted Flora into a room hung with glinting tapestries. A man was sitting at the head of a long table, and Flora saw he was holding a marvellous pear.

"You've been welcome here," said the man. "And this pear is for you. You must not break it or open it until you have great need of it."

Again the castle servants lifted Flora on to the bull's back. Away they went, and they travelled many, many miles. Flora had never seen such a desolate place: one moment she was squinting up at a towering rockface, the next peering over the edge of a precipice. The bull hurried on and in the evening they came to a third castle: it was made entirely of painted and decorated wood.

"That's where we'll stay tonight," the bull said. "My youngest brother lives there."

"Who are you, then?" said Flora.

But the bull did not reply; he galloped up to the castle courtyard.

Servants lifted Flora down from the bull's back, and ushered the bull into a pasture for the night. Then, in the morning, a servant conducted Flora into a room with mirror walls. A man was sitting at the head of a table and Flora saw he was holding a wonderful plum.

"You've been welcome here," said the man. "And this plum is for you. You must not open it or break it until you have great need of it."

Once again, the castle servants lifted Flora on to the bull's back. Away they went until they came to a dark and ugsome valley. Soaring rock shoulders rose up on either side of a fast-running stream, blocking out all but the mid-day sun, and the stream itself was littered with boulders.

"This is the place," said the black bull. "Get down from my back."

Flora dismounted and looked up at the black bull, his broad shoulders, his bloodshot eyes and matted rough hair.

"You must wait here," said the bull, "while I go on and fight the devil. You must sit on that rock."

Flora looked at the saucer-shaped rock lying half in and half out of the water.

"Sit on that rock and move neither hand nor foot until I come back! If you move even once, I'll never be able to find you. If everything around you turns blue, I'll have beaten the devil," said the bull. "But if everything turns red, he'll have beaten me."

Flora sat down on the saucer-shaped rock. She stared at the water; she dreamed of her mother and sisters, so far away; and she wondered about her travelling companion . . .

After a while, everything around Flora began to turn blue. The high rock shoulders turned indigo, and the rocks in the stream turned slate-blue; the silver water turned aquamarine and the clouds parted overhead.

Flora cried out in delight. She wanted to shout and to dance. She lifted her left foot and crossed it over her right foot.

When the black bull came back to the dark valley, he was unable to find Flora. She heard him and called out to him again and again. But he could neither see her nor hear her.

In the end Flora stood up. Without knowing where she was going, she walked on up the valley. Now and then she glimpsed a shining peak far ahead and, as she drew closer to it, Flora saw it was made entirely of glass.

"If I can climb this mountain," Flora said to herself, "I'll see how the land lies. I need food and shelter. Unless I climb this mountain, I'll never find my way home."

But Flora wasn't able to climb the mountain. She couldn't get more than a few feet up its steep side before she slid down to the bottom again.

Flora began to sob. Slowly she picked her way across the scree and round the foot of the glass mountain. And that evening, on the fringe of a pinewood, she came across a mountain hut. It was little more than a large shed and at first Flora thought it was deserted. But then an old man got up and hobbled towards her.

The man saw that Flora was so tired she could scarcely speak or eat or drink. He gave her a bowl of soup and asked her no questions. "You can sleep here," he said, pointing to a piece of dirty sacking.

Flora slept, and in the morning she learned that the old man was a smith, and asked for his help. "Unless I can climb the glass mountain," she said, "I'll never find my way home."

"I'll help you if you help me," said the old man. "If you work for me for seven years, I'll make you a pair of iron shoes, and with those you'll be able to climb over the mountain."

After seven years, Flora got her iron shoes and climbed over the glass mountain. She could see around her a great spread of peaks and glaciers and high grazing pastures and forests and valleys. The whole country was at her feet. She looked and she looked and at last she picked out her way home.

Flora walked for eight days. And on the ninth day she reached her own mountain slopes, and stopped at the cottage of the wise woman.

"Ah! So you've come back," said the wise woman, "and maybe just in time. A young knight and his two hunting companions are taking shelter here for a few days. The knight has given me these bloodstained shirts to wash. 'And whoever washes these shirts clean,' that's what he said, 'whoever washes these shirts clean will be my wife'."

"And you cannot wash them?" asked Flora.

"I cannot," said the woman. "And my daughter cannot."

"Then how can I?"

"I can read things that will happen," the wise woman said. "Try to wash them!"

So Flora warmed a bucket of water over the fire and washed the shirts. One by one, the stains disappeared.

"The shirts are spotless," said the wise woman.

"Then this knight and I will be married," said Flora.

But Flora was so tired after her adventures that, while she was waiting for the young knight to return that evening, she fell asleep. The wise woman welcomed the knight, and told him that her own daughter had washed the shirts clean, and he agreed to marry her.

When Flora woke, she saw she was lying on the wise woman's bed. First she spied how handsome the knight was, with his bull-neck and broad shoulders and black hair. "I know you," Flora whispered to herself. "I know who you are. And now I know why for seven years I have worked and walked and waited."

But then Flora heard him and the wise woman discussing plans for a wedding between the knight and the woman's own daughter—and it was to take place that very evening. She felt alone and very unhappy. She felt in great need.

"My apple," she whispered.

Flora broke open the apple and found it was full of gold and fine jewellery. Then she called out to the wise woman's daughter.

"You're awake then," said the daughter.

"You see this?" said Flora.

The wise woman's daughter gazed at the jewellery and her mouth dropped open.

"And you're going to marry that knight?" said Flora.

"You can't stop me," said the daughter.

"I'll give you all this," said Flora, "if you put off the wedding until tomorrow, and let me go into his room alone tonight."

The daughter agreed, but when the wise woman heard of the arrangement, she mixed a sleeping potion into the knight's ale. Then she and her daughter laid out the knight in their own bedroom and settled down to sleep beside the fire.

Flora crept in and stared at the sleeping knight, his bull-neck and broad shoulders and black hair. "I know who you are," she said to herself. "I know who you are." Then she sat down beside him and softly began to sing:

"Seven long years I worked for you,
The glass mountain I climbed for you,
The bloodstained shirt I wrung for you;
And will you not wake and turn to me?"

But the knight did not wake; he did not even stir. Flora began to weep and to sing again, but the knight slept until daylight.

Next morning, Flora broke open the pear. It was full of jewellery even more precious than that in the apple. With these jewels she bargained for a second time with the wise woman's daughter. And that night, after the knight had returned with his two hunting companions, and they had all eaten together, Flora again crept into the room where the knight was asleep. With the soft voice of a dove, she sang:

"Seven long years I worked for you,
The glass mountain I climbed for you,
The bloodstained shirt I wrung for you;
And will you not wake and turn to me?"

Again and again she sang, she sobbed and she sang, but the knight did not wake; he did not even stir. The wise woman had given him another sleeping potion.

In the morning, the knight and his companions went off hunting again, promising to return in time for the celebration of the wedding that evening.

"What was that noise?" asked one companion. "All last night, that cooing and moaning?"

"I heard nothing," the knight said.

"In your room," said the other companion. "Singing and sobbing."

"That's strange," said the knight. "I'll take no chances tonight. I want to keep awake and hear these sounds for myself."

Flora lived in hope and despair. She broke open the plum; it held by far the most valuable jewellery of all. Once more she bargained with the wise woman's daughter; and for a third time the wise woman mixed a sleeping potion into the knight's ale.

"To tell you the truth," said the knight, "I've a sweet tooth, and this ale's rather sour! Will you get me some honey to sweeten it?"

While the wise woman went out for some honey, the knight quickly poured the ale into the rushes in one corner of the room and refilled his wooden mug with water from the pitcher.

"There!" said the wise woman. "This will sweeten it."

Then the knight retired to his bedroom, and his two companions and the wise woman and her daughter spread themselves out around the fire. Before long, Flora returned to the knight's room for the third time. With the clear voice of a nightingale, she began to sing:

> "Seven long years I worked for you,
> The glass mountain I climbed for you,
> The bloodstained shirt I wrung for you;
> And will you not wake and turn to me?"

The young knight heard and he turned to Flora. She told him all that had befallen her then, and he told her all that had happened to him.

The knight did not wait until morning. He stood up and ordered his companions to truss the treacherous old woman and her daughter and burn them to death.

Day dawned. Flora led the knight up through the pine forest and over the slopes of the mountain. At the door of the cottage far above, her mother was standing and watching and waiting.

Before long, the knight and Flora were married. How happy they were! And for all I know, how happy they are!

THE PIPER AND THE POOKA

The only tune that Patsy could play was Black Rogue. He put a pillow of wind in his bagpipe and he played it loud and played it soft; he played it for all he was worth and on every occasion.

The trouble was that Patsy was as dim as a donkey. Much as he loved music and dancing, he was unable to learn more than one tune. When at a dance some strutting cockerel or eye-bright hen called on him to play another tune, he'd smile and strike it up only to frown and break off after a few snatches, shaking his head and muttering to himself, "It's gone. Where's it gone?"

Late one night, Patsy was walking home after playing at a dance in a neighbouring village. It wasn't too friendly a way, what with hanging rocks on either side of the road, and it wasn't too friendly a night — dungeon-dark and the November wind whistling sharp and out of tune.

Weaving down the tiddly road and warbling to himself,

Patsy felt a little lonely; and when he reached the hump-backed bridge, he was still two miles out from the village of Dunmore and the warmth of his mother's cottage. So he unstrung his pipes and put wind in the bag and began to play.

Up behind the piper crept a shape. The shape had horns. First it was two-legged, now it was four-legged. It grinned and it lowered its head.

"Wowk!" shouted Patsy, as first he felt the horns jammed against his buttocks and then he lost his footing and was tossed into the air.

Patsy did a backwards somersault and landed on the creature's back. He got a good grip on its horns and yelled, "The devil take you, you nasty beast! Let me go home!"

"Never mind home," said the creature.

"I've been playing all night," shouted Patsy. "I've got a sixpenny piece for my pains, and it's for my mother."

"Never mind your mother!" said the creature.

"She needs it to buy snuff," cried Patsy.

"Stuff!" replied the creature. "You just keep a hold on my horns. If you fall off, you'll break your pipes — and you'll break your neck too."

So Patsy gripped the creature's shaggy back with his knees and before long, as they trotted along, it said, "Play up, Patsy! Play Poor Old Woman for me."

"How can I do that?" said Patsy. "I've never heard of it."

"Never mind whether you have or you haven't," said the creature. "You play up and I'll see you know it."

So the piper put wind in his bag and he began to play. Oh! The darkness lightened and clouds danced in front of the moon; the sharp-tongued wind stood back. Patsy played high and low, simple and intricate. All the listening cows and rabbits and sheep pawed at the ground and stamped, all of them longing to be part of the dance.

At last Patsy came to the end of the tune. The pipes wheezed and fell silent and Patsy took a deep breath. "My!" he said. "You're a fine music master."

The creature said nothing. It kept trotting forward at a steady pace, untroubled by the dark or the piper on its back.

"Where are we going?" asked Patsy. "Will you tell me that?"

"There's a great feast tonight," said the creature, "in the house of the weeping women."

"Where's that, then?" asked Patsy.

"Up on top of the holy mountain," said the creature. "Croagh Patrick."

"Is that right?" said Patsy. "You're saving me a journey, then. I stole Father William's white gander at Martinmas. And when he found out, he told me my penance was to go to Croagh Patrick."

Now the creature increased the length of his step, and broke into a kind of canter. Round rugged outcrops and over squelching peat bogs, into tapering valleys and up steep slopes—on they went until at last they came to the top of Croagh Patrick.

The creature stopped. He struck the ground three times with one hoof. Then in the half-light Patsy saw a great rock door slowly open, and at once the creature passed through it with the piper still on his back. They entered a great shining hall.

Patsy let go of the creature's horns and slipped off its back and looked about him. In the middle of the room stood a huge table, much the largest Patsy had ever seen in his life, and it looked as if it were made from gold.

Round the table sat a crowd of old women, there must have been hundreds of them—and all of them had long hair, and eyes red as firecoals from wailing and weeping. They wore green dresses and grey cloaks.

Now there was a great scraping and rustling. The women stood up and called out, "A thousand thousand welcomes to you, Pooka of November! Who is this you've brought with you?"

"The best piper in Ireland," said the Pooka.

One of the old women stepped towards Patsy, and struck the ground with her stick. At once a little door in the rock wall opened, and out stepped a white gander, the same that Patsy had stolen from Father William.

"My!" said Patsy. "By my conscience, I ate this gander!" The piper eyed the bird and the bird eyed Patsy. "My mother and I, we ate every piece of him — all except one wing, and I gave that to Red Mary. The devil take her, it's she told Father William . . ."

But now the gander seemed to have lost interest in Patsy. It paddled away and started to clear the plates and goblets from the table.

"Now, Patsy," said the Pooka, "you must play up! Play a tune for these ladies."

So Patsy played Black Rogue, the only tune he knew, and the old women began to dance — backward and forward and round and round, their grey hair and white hair streaming out behind them. But then Patsy struck up a second tune and a third, a whole succession of tunes which, like Poor Old Woman, he'd never even heard of before. The old women danced until they were too tired to dance any longer.

"Pay the piper, ladies!" shouted the Pooka, grinning from ear to ear. "Pay the piper!" The old women stumbled and fumbled as each and every one of them found a gold coin in a purse, or hidden pocket, and gave it to Patsy.

"Bags of it!" brayed Patsy. "By the tooth of St. Patrick, I'm as rich as the son of a lord."

"Come with me," said the Pooka. "I'll take you home."

Patsy and the Pooka turned towards the door and, just as the piper was about to mount once more on the creature's back, the white gander prinked up to Patsy and presented him with a brand new set of pipes.

"That's very handsome," said Patsy. "Very civil! I wish I hadn't eaten you."

It wasn't long before the Pooka brought Patsy back to the little hump-backed bridge only two miles outside the village of Dunmore.

"Go home, Patsy!" said the creature, and its black eyes gleamed in the light of dawn. "You've got two things now you didn't have before."

"What's that?" asked Patsy.

"Some wits between your two ears," said the Pooka, "and a memory for music."

So Patsy strode home to his mother's cottage and, in the first pale green light, banged on the door. And when his sleeping mother took more than a moment to rouse herself, Patsy banged again and bawled, "Let me in! Let me in! I'm as rich as a lord and the best piper in Ireland."

"I'll tell you what you are," said Patsy's mother. "You're as drunk as a lord, and a rogue into the bargain."

"Not at all," said Patsy. "I haven't drunk a drop. Not a drop since midnight."

Patsy's mother opened the door and let her son in. Then she crossed the little room and knelt down in front of the dozy fire and cupped her hands and began to blow at the peats.

"Look!" said Patsy, emptying his pockets. "There!" he shouted, as the gold pieces ran all over the floor.

"Patsy!" cried his mother. "Where in heaven's name . . ." The old woman scrambled to left and to right, gathering up all the pieces of gold so that they lay in one shining pool in her lap.

"And these new pipes!" said Patsy proudly. "Wait now till you hear the music I play."

Patsy buckled on the pipes and filled the bag with wind. But what music! Instead of responding to his quick fingers, the pipes made a hideous cackling, as if all the ganders and geese in Ireland were tucked inside them and cackling together.

"Stop!" shouted Patsy's mother. "Stop!"

Patsy needed no encouragement. He unstrapped the pipes and put them in the corner of the little room. But the terrible racket had already woken up all the neighbours in the surrounding cottages. Tipsy with sleep and tousled, they came stumbling through the door one after another, first indignant, then curious, then mocking.

"I'll put on my old pipes then," said Patsy stubbornly.

"And play Black Rogue!" said several voices, none too kindly. "Black Rogue, Patsy! Is that what you'll do?"

But Patsy did not play Black Rogue. He closed his eyes and opened his eyes and his fingers remembered all the dances and every note that he played for the weeping women on the top of Croagh Patrick.

"And then there's this," said Patsy's mother slyly, untying the shawl in which she had secreted all the gold, and laying it out in front of her friends and neighbours.

Then Patsy himself sat down in front of the laughing fire and told them everything that had happened since he left the dance the previous night. "All of it," he said, "while you were asleep. All of it between midnight and first light."

After they had eaten later that morning, Patsy's mother had a peep into the shawl for the second time. It was full of crackling leaves, nothing but November leaves, russet and gold and brown.

"Ah! Patsy!" said his mother sadly, and with one clump of a fist she covered her eyes.

Then Patsy went to find Father William and told him everything that had happened the previous night.

Father William shook his head. He kept shaking his head and he smiled. "Cock and bull!" he said. "Claptrap, Patsy! And you know it."

"It's true," said Patsy, indignantly. "I'll show you. I'll put these pipes on me." He buckled on the new pipes and filled the bag till it was bursting. Once more the pipes made a horrible honking and screeching.

"Get out, you thief!" shouted Father William.

"And now these," said Patsy, as soon as the caterwauling had died away.

"Out!" shouted Father William. "Away with you! And off to Croagh Patrick!"

But Patsy stood his ground and fastened on his old pipes. And then what music he played! First he played well-known tunes, and then the unfamiliar tunes he had played for the weeping women at the top of the mountain—and all with neat fingering and fine phrasing, true to the circle of the dance.

The old priest clicked his fingers and inside his shiny black shoes his toes began to tingle. Little birds looked in at his window.

And from that day until the day he died, Patsy was hailed as prince of pipers in the county of Galway.

THE SMALL-TOOTH DOG

The youth put a scowling fist in Mr. Markham's face. "The cash!" he growled.

The second and third youths stood behind Mr. Markham; they said nothing.

So the poor man had no choice. On the corner of his own street, only a hundred yards from the safety of his own home, he miserably fished in his pocket. But while Mr. Markham was delving for his wallet and loose change, a big dog, brindled and shaggy, came trotting round the corner.

"Help!" shouted Mr. Markham, and he punched one youth in the stomach and elbowed another in the face.

The big brindled dog leaped into the scrum. He ripped the youths' clothes, he bit their calves and arms until they yelped and yelled and ran off. Mr. Markham was left lying on the pavement, a poor fat bundle, his head cradled in his arms.

The big brindled dog gave him a friendly look and Mr.

Markham began to unfold and put himself together again. He looked at his cuts and bruises; he looked at the dog and shook his head.

"You've saved me a packet," he said, clasping a hand over the inner pocket of his jacket, "I've got the week's takings in here. More than a thousand pounds."

"I know," said the dog.

"Ah!" said Mr. Markham, and he gave the big brindled dog another, careful look. The dog bared its teeth in a kind of smile and Mr. Markham saw that they were surprisingly white and neat and small for such a large, shaggy animal.

"Well!" said Mr. Markham. "I'd like to repay you for your kindness. You've saved me a fortune."

"I've saved your life," said the dog, sitting back comfortably on his haunches.

"So I'm going to give you my most precious possession," said Mr. Markham.

"What's that?" asked the dog.

"How would you like the fish?" said Mr. Markham. "It can speak Welsh and Portugese and Bulgarian and Icelandic and . . ."

"I would not," said the dog.

"What about the goose, then?" said Mr. Markham. "Would you like the goose? It lays golden eggs."

"I would not," said the dog.

"Well then," said Mr. Markham slowly, "I'll have to offer you the mirror . . ."

"The mirror?" said the dog.

"If you look into it," said Mr. Markham, "you can see what people are thinking."

"I've no need of that," said the big brindled dog.

"What would you like, then?" said Mr. Markham.

"Nothing like that," replied the dog. "I'll take your daughter. I'll take her back to my house."

"Corinna!" cried Mr. Markham. "Well! A man must keep his word. My most precious possession."

"Me?" cried Corinna. "Not likely!"

"He's not an ordinary dog," said Mr. Markham.

"You're daft as a brush," said Corinna.

"You'll see," said her father. "He's waiting outside the door."

"Crazy!" said Corinna.

"Go on!" said Mr. Markham.

"Never!" said Corinna.

"You'll have to go, Corinna," her father said. "I want you to humour him. Take him for a walk." Mr. Markham smiled encouragingly. You'll be back again for tea." Then he bustled his half-laughing, half-fearful daughter into her coat and out of the front door.

"Corinna!" said the big brindled dog. "On my back! I'm taking you back to my house."

As soon as Corinna had mounted, the big brindled dog galloped off down the road, leaving Mr. Markham standing and staring after them. The dog galloped over the Common and down the grey November streets. He galloped until they were right out of the city. And at last, in the middle of a beechwood on the brow of a hill, they came to the dog's house.

"Here we are!" said the big brindled dog. "You'll like it here."

Corinna didn't like it at all. She didn't like the big brindled dog. She didn't like leaving home. She didn't like the countryside. And she didn't like the dog's damp draughty house.

The dog brought Corinna good things to eat; he promised to look after her; he sang her praises. But whatever he did seemed only to make Corinna more miserable. And one night, when she had been at the dog's house for about a month, Corinna began to shake and sob in her sleep, and she woke up already weeping.

"What's wrong with you?" asked the dog.

"Let me go home!" sobbed Corinna. "I want to go home. My dad! He's got no one to look after him."

"I'll take you home," said the big brindled dog, "if you promise not to stay more than three days."

"Three days!" cried Corinna.

"That's it," said the dog.

"You're a great, foul, small-tooth dog," said Corinna.

"All right," said the dog. "I won't take you home."

But Corinna begged and wept and wailed, and at last the dog relented. "We'll be on our way at once," he said. "What did you say you called me?"

"You?" said Corinna, and she flashed her dark eyes. "You're sweet-as-a-honeycomb."

"On my back!" said the dog. "I'll take you home."

The big brindled dog with Corinna on his back trotted along for mile after mile. They crossed major roads and minor roads and fields and streams. Then they came to a stile.

"Just remind me what you call me," said the dog.

Corinna was thinking of her dad and her own room and her job and her friends. "You're a great, foul, small-tooth dog," she said.

When he heard this, the big brindled dog turned his back on the stile. Deaf to all Corinna's cries and promises, he trotted straight back to the beechwood on the brow of the hill.

Corinna had learned her lesson. And when, a week later, only just in time for Christmas, she once again persuaded the big brindled dog to take her home, she made up her mind to say nothing but loving things — the most loving things she could think of — until she was safely home.

"Sweet-as-a-honeycomb," she said before they set off. And "sweet-as-a-honeycomb" again at the stile. And in the dog's pricked ears for mile after mile, "Sugar . . . sweetie . . . honey."

It was already dark as they rounded the corner where the big brindled dog had rescued Mr. Markham from the three youths. The dog quickened into a canter.

"This one," cried Corinna. "The red one!" she cried, half-joyful at getting home at last, half-angry with the dog for having taken her away for so long. She dismounted and stepped up to the front door.

"Just remind me what you call me," said the big brindled dog.

"You," said Corinna, "you're a great . . ."

But then she saw the dog's mournful look. With her hand on the cold doorknob, Corinna thought of how, during the past weeks, the dog had always been warm and kind and patient with her, and put up with her tempers and tears. The word "foul" stuck in her throat. "Sweeter-than-a-honeycomb," said Corinna, and she smiled.

The big brindled dog stood up on his hind legs. He put his forelegs to the sides of his great shaggy head, and pulled his head off. He pulled it off and tossed it high in the air. Then he took off his hairy coat. And there he stood, a young man, cool and smiling, and just dandy. He had the smallest teeth you ever saw.

So when Corinna turned the cold doorknob, and stepped into the house, the young man stepped in after her.

"Dad!" shouted Corinna.

A few months later, on the Saturday before Easter, the church bells rang and Corinna and her dog-man got married.

"Crazy!" said Corinna.

THE THREE BLOWS

Their stone farmhouse seemed to grow out of the grey-green skirt of the mountain. The walls were lichenous, one part of the roof was covered with slate and the other part with turf. The whole building was so low slung it seemed to be crouching.

It wasn't alone. Megan could stand at their door (you had to stoop to get in or out) and see three other small-holdings within reach, almost within shouting distance. And no more than a mile away, along the track north and west, huddled and patient, was the little village of Llan-ddeusant.

But when the wind opened its throat and rain swept across the slopes; when the lean seasons came to Black Mountain; when wolves circled the pens and small birds left their sanskrit in the snow: the farm seemed alone then, alone in the world—and all the more so to Megan since her husband had died leaving her to bring up their baby son and run the farm on her own.

But Megan was a hard-working woman. As the years passed, her holding of cattle and sheep and goats so increased that they strayed far and wide over Black Mountain. And all the while her son grew and grew until he became a big-boned young man: rather awkward, very strong-willed, and shy and affectionate. Yet sometimes, when she looked at him sitting by the fire, lost in his own sliding dreams, it seemed to Megan that she didn't really quite know her son. *He's like his father*, she thought. *Something hidden. What is he thinking?*

Gwyn spent most of his time up on Black Mountain, herding the cattle and sheep and goats. More often than not he followed them up to a remote place in a fold of the mountain: it was a secret eye, a dark pupil that watched the sun and moon and stars: the little lake of Llyn y Fan Fach.

One spring morning, Gwyn was poking along the edge of the lake, on his way to the flat rock where he sometimes sat and spread out his provisions — barley-bread, maybe, and a chump of cheese, a wooden bottle seething with ale. Gwyn clambered on to the rock and stared out across the lake, silver and obsidian. And there, sitting on the glassy surface of the water, combing her hair, he saw a young woman. She was using the water as a mirror, charming her hair into ringlets, arranging them so that they covered her shoulders; and only when she had finished did she look up and see Gwyn, awkward on the rock, open-mouthed, arms stretched out, offering her bread . . .

Slowly, so slowly she scarcely seemed to move at all, the young woman glided over the surface of the water towards Gwyn and, entranced, he stepped down to meet her.

And then Gwyn heard her voice. It was like a bell heard long ago and remembered: very sweet and very low.

"Your bread's baked and hard," she said. "It's not easy to catch me."

Which is just what Gwyn tried to do. He lunged into the lake, and at once the girl sank from sight; she left her smile behind, playing on the smooth surface of the water.

For a while Gwyn stood and stared. A stray cloud passed in front of the sun; the water shivered. Gwyn felt as if he had found the one thing in this world that mattered only to lose it. And he resolved to come back, to find the girl and catch her, whatever the cost.

Gwyn turned away from the lake. He set off down the string-thin sheep-runs, the network that covered the steep shoulders of the mountain. At first he walked slowly, but by the time he reached the doors of his farmhouse he was almost running, so eager was he to tell his mother about the bewitching girl he had seen up at Llyn y Fan Fach.

"Stuff!" said Megan. "You and your dreams." But as she listened to Gwyn, she did not doubt that he was telling the truth. Perhaps she saw in the young man at her hearth another young man at the same hearth long before, shining and stammering. But then she quailed as she thought of what might become of Gwyn if he was caught up with the fairy folk.

"I won't be put off," said Gwyn. "I won't be put off if that's what you're thinking."

"Leave her alone, Gwyn," said Megan. "Take a girl from the valley."

"I won't be put off," said Gwyn.

"You won't catch her," Megan said, "not unless you listen to me."

"What do you mean?" said Gwyn.

"'Your bread's baked and hard.' Isn't that what she said?"

Gwyn nodded.

"Well, then. Take up some toes. Take up some toes. Stands to reason."

"Toes?" said Gwyn.

"Pieces of dough. Unbaked and just as they are."

Gwyn followed his mother's advice. As night began to lose its thickness, yet before you could say it was dawn, he filled one pocket with dough, and quietly let himself out of the farmhouse without waking his mother. He sniffed the cool air and began to climb the dun and misty mountain.

She was not there. Shape-changing mist that plays tricks with the eyes dipped and rose and dipped over the dark water until the sun came down from the peaks and burned it away. Birds arrived in boating parties, little fish made circles, and she was not there.

Not long before dusk, Gwyn saw that two of his cows were lumbering straight towards the top of the dangerous escarpment on the far side of the lake. He stood up at once and began to run round the lake after them. "Stupids!" he bawled. "You'll lose your footing."

Then she was there. She was there, sitting on the shimmer of the water, smiling, just as she had done on the day before.

Gwyn stopped. He reached out his arms and, as the beautiful young woman drifted towards him, he gazed at her: the blue-black sheen of her hair, her long fingers, the green watersilk of her dress, and her little ankles and sandals tied with thongs. Then Gwyn dug into his pockets and offered her the unbaked dough and not only that but his hand too and his heart for ever.

"Your bread is unbaked," said the young woman. "I will not have you." Then she raised her arms and sank under the surface of the water.

Gwyn cried out, and the rockface heard and answered him, all hollow and disembodied. But even as he looked at the lake and listened to the sounds, each as mournful as the other, Gwyn thought of the girl's smile and was half-comforted. "I'll catch you," he said.

"You caught the cows," said Megan later that evening. "That's what matters."

Gwyn grinned.

"Anyhow," said Megan, "you're not going up there again, are you?"

"You know I am," said Gwyn.

"In that case," said his mother, "listen to me. I'd take some partly baked bread up with you."

Gwyn reached Llyn y Fan Fach again as day dawned. He kept a watch on the lake and his whole face glowed—his cheeks and chin and ears and eyes, above all his eyes—as if he had just turned away from a leaping fire. He felt strong and he felt weak.

This time it was the sheep and goats that strayed towards the rockface and scree at the far end of the lake. But Gwyn knew how nimble-footed they were. Even when they loosened and dislodged a rock that bumped and bundled down the escarpment and splashed into the lake, they were in no danger.

All morning wayward April shook sheets of sunlight and rain over the lake and then, in the afternoon, the clouds piling in from the west closed over the mountain. For hour after hour, Gwyn crouched on the smooth rock or padded round the rim of the lake. Now he was no longer so excited or fearful; the long waiting had dulled him.

In the early evening, the mood of the weather changed

again. First Gwyn could see blue sky behind the gauze of cloud, and then the clouds left the mountain altogether. The lake and the ashen scree were soothed by yellow sunlight.

This was the hour when Gwyn saw that three cows were walking on the water. They were out in the middle of Llyn y Fan Fach and ambling towards him.

Gwyn stood up. He swung off the rock platform and down to the lakeside. And as he did so, the young woman appeared for the third time, as beautiful as before, passing over the mirror of water just behind the three cows.

Gwyn stepped into the lake, up to his shins, his thighs, his hips. Still the young woman came on, and she was smiling—an expression that lit up her whole face, and above all her violet eyes.

Gwyn reached out his hands and, wordless, offered her the partly baked bread.

The young woman took the bread, and Gwyn grasped her cool hand. He was nervous and breathless.

"Come with me," he said. "Come to the farm . . . I'll show you. Come with me . . . marry me!"

The young woman looked at Gwyn.

"I'll not let you go," said Gwyn. He could hear his voice rising, as if someone else were speaking. "I've waited!" He tightened his grip on the girl's hand.

"Gwyn," said the young woman. "I will marry you," she said, "on one condition."

"Anything!" said Gwyn. "Anything you ask."

"I will marry you and live with you. But if you strike me . . ."

"Strike you!" cried Gwyn.

". . . strike me three blows without reason, I'll return to this lake and you'll never see me again."

"Never!" swore Gwyn. "Never!" He loosened his fierce grip and at once she slid away, raised her arms, and disappeared under the surface of the water.

"Come back!" shouted Gwyn. "Come back!"

"Gon-ba!" said the mountain. "Gon-ba!"

Gwyn stood up to his waist in the chill water. The huge, red sun alighted on the western horizon and began to slip out of sight.

But now two young women, each as lovely as the other, rose out of the water and a tall old white-headed man immediately after them. At once they came walking towards Gwyn.

"Greetings, Gwyn!" called the old man. "You mean to marry one of my daughters, you've asked her to marry you." He waved towards the two girls at his side. "And I agree to this. You can marry her if you can tell me which one you mean to marry."

Gwyn looked from one girl to the other: their clefs of black hair, their strange violet eyes, their long necks . . .

One of the girls tossed her charcoal hair; the other eased one foot forward, one inch, two inches, and into Gwyn's memory. The sandals . . . the thongs . . .

Gwyn reached out at once across the water and took her cool hand. "This is she," he said.

"You have made your choice?" asked the old man.

"I have," said Gwyn.

"You've chosen well," the man said. "And you can marry her. Be kind to her, and faithful."

"I will," said Gwyn, "and I will."

"This is her dowry," said the man. "She can have as many sheep and cattle and goats and horses as she can count without drawing breath."

No sooner had her father spoken than his daughter

began to count for the sheep. She counted in fives, "One, two, three, four, five — one, two, three, four, five" over and over again until she'd run out of breath.

"Thirty-two times," said the man. "One hundred and sixty sheep." As soon as they had been named, the sheep appeared on the surface of the darkening water, and ran across it to the bare mountain.

"Now the cattle," said the old man. Then his daughter began to count again, her voice soft and rippling. And so they went on until there were more than six hundred head of sheep and cattle and goats and horses milling around on the lakeside.

"Go now," said the white-headed man gently. "And remember, Gwyn, if you strike her three blows without reason, she'll return to me, and bring all her livestock back to this lake."

It was almost dark. The old man and his other daughter went down into the lake. Gwyn took his bride's hand and, followed by her livestock, led her down from the mountain.

So Gwyn and the girl from Llan y Fan Fach were married. Gwyn left the house in which he had been born, and his mother in it, and went to a farm a few miles away, outside the village of Myddfai.

Gwyn and his wife were happy and, because of the generosity of the old man, they were rich. They had three sons, dark-haired, dark-eyed, lovely to look at.

Some years after Gwyn and his wife had moved to Myddfai, they were invited to a christening back in Llan-ddeusant. Gwyn was eager to go but, when the time came for them to set off, his wife was not.

"I don't know these people," she said.

"It's Gareth," said Gwyn. "I've known him all my life. And this is his first child."

"It's too far to walk," said his wife.

"Fetch a horse from the field then," said Gwyn. "You can ride down."

"Will you go and find my gloves," said Gwyn's wife, "while I get the horse? I left them in the house."

When Gwyn came out of the farmhouse with the gloves, eager to be off, his wife had made no move towards the paddock and the horse.

"What's wrong?" cried Gwyn, and he slapped his wife's shoulder with one of her gloves.

Gwyn's wife turned to face him. Her eyes darkened. "Gwyn!" she said. "Gwyn! Remember the condition on which I married you."

"I remember," said Gwyn.

"That you would never strike me without reason."

Gwyn nodded.

"Be careful! Be more careful from now on!"

Not long after this, Gwyn and his wife went to a fine wedding. The guests at the breakfast came not only from Llanddeusant and Myddfai but many of the surrounding farms and villages. The barn in which the reception was held was filled with the hum of contentment and the sweet sound of the triple harp.

As soon as she had kissed the bride, Gwyn's wife began to weep and then to sob. The guests around her stopped talking. A few tried to comfort her but many backed away, superstitious of tears at a wedding.

Gwyn didn't know quite what to do. "What's wrong?" he whispered. "What's wrong?" But his wife sobbed as bitterly as a little child. Gwyn smiled apologetically and shook his head; then he pursed his lips and dropped a hand on to his wife's arm. "What's the matter?" he insisted. "You must stop!"

Gwyn's wife gazed at her husband with her flooded violet eyes. "These two people," she said, "are on the threshold of such trouble. I see it all. And Gwyn," she said, "I see your troubles are about to begin. You've struck me without reason for the second time."

Gwyn's wife loved her husband no less than he loved her and neither had the least desire that their marriage should suddenly come to an end. Knowing that her own behaviour could surprise and upset Gwyn, she sometimes reminded her husband to be very careful not to strike her for a third time. "Otherwise," she said, "I must return to Llyn y Fan Fach. I have no choice in the matter."

But the years passed. The three boys became young men, all of them intelligent. And when he thought about it at all, Gwyn believed that he had learned his lesson on the way to the christening and at the wedding, and that he and his water-wife would live together happily for as long as they lived.

One day, Gwyn and his wife went to a funeral. Everyone round about had come to pay their last respects to the dead woman: she had been the daughter of a rich farmer and wife to the priest, generous with her time and money, and still in the prime of her life.

After the funeral, a good number of the priest's friends went back to his house to eat funeral cakes with him and keep him company, and Gwyn and his wife were among them.

No sooner had they stepped inside the priest's house than Gwyn's wife began to laugh. Amongst the mourners with their black suits and sober faces, she giggled as if she were tipsy with ale or romping with young children.

Gwyn was shocked. "Shush!" he said. "Think where you are! Stop this laughing!" he said. And firmly he laid a restraining hand on his wife's forearm.

"I'm laughing," said Gwyn's wife, "because when a person dies, she passes out of this world of trouble. Ah! Gwyn," she cried, "you've struck me for the third time and the last time. Our marriage is at an end."

Gwyn's wife left the funeral feast alone and went straight back to their fine farm outside Myddfai. There she began to call in all her livestock.

"Brindled cow, come! White speckled cow, spotted cow, bold freckled cow, come! Old white-faced cow, Grey Squinter, white bull from the court of the king, come and come home!"

Gwyn's wife knew each of her livestock by name. And she did not forget the calf her husband had slaughtered only the previous week. "Little black calf," she cried, "come down from the hook! Come home!"

The black calf leaped into life; it danced around the courtyard.

Then Gwyn's wife saw four of her oxen ploughing a nearby field. "Grey oxen!" she cried. "Four oxen of the field, you too must come home!"

When they heard her, the oxen turned from their task and, for all the whistles of the ploughboy, dragged the plough right across the newly turned furrows.

Gwyn's wife looked about her. She paused. Then she turned her back on the farmhouse and the farm. Those who saw her never forgot that sight: one woman, sad and steadfast, walking up on to Myddfai mountain, and behind her, plodding and trudging and tripping and high-stepping, a great concourse of creatures.

The woman crossed over on to the swept slopes of Black

Mountain just above the lonely farm where Gwyn had been born and where Megan still lived in her old age. Up she climbed, on and up to the dark eye.

The Lady of Llyn y Fan Fach walked over the surface of the water and disappeared into the water, and all her hundreds of animals followed her. They left behind them sorrow, they left a wake of silence, and the deep furrow made by the oxen as they dragged their plough up over the shoulder of the mountain and into the lake.

BOO!

She didn't like it at all when her father had to go down to London and, for the first time, she had to sleep alone in the old house.

She went up to her bedroom early. She turned the key and locked the door. She latched the windows and drew the curtains. Then she peered inside her wardrobe, and pulled open the bottom drawer of her clothes press; she got down on her knees and looked under the bed.

She undressed; she put on her nightdress.

She pulled back the heavy linen cover and climbed into bed. Not to read but to try and sleep — she wanted to sleep as soon as she could. She reached out and turned off the lamp.

"That's good," said a little voice. "Now we're safely locked in for the night."